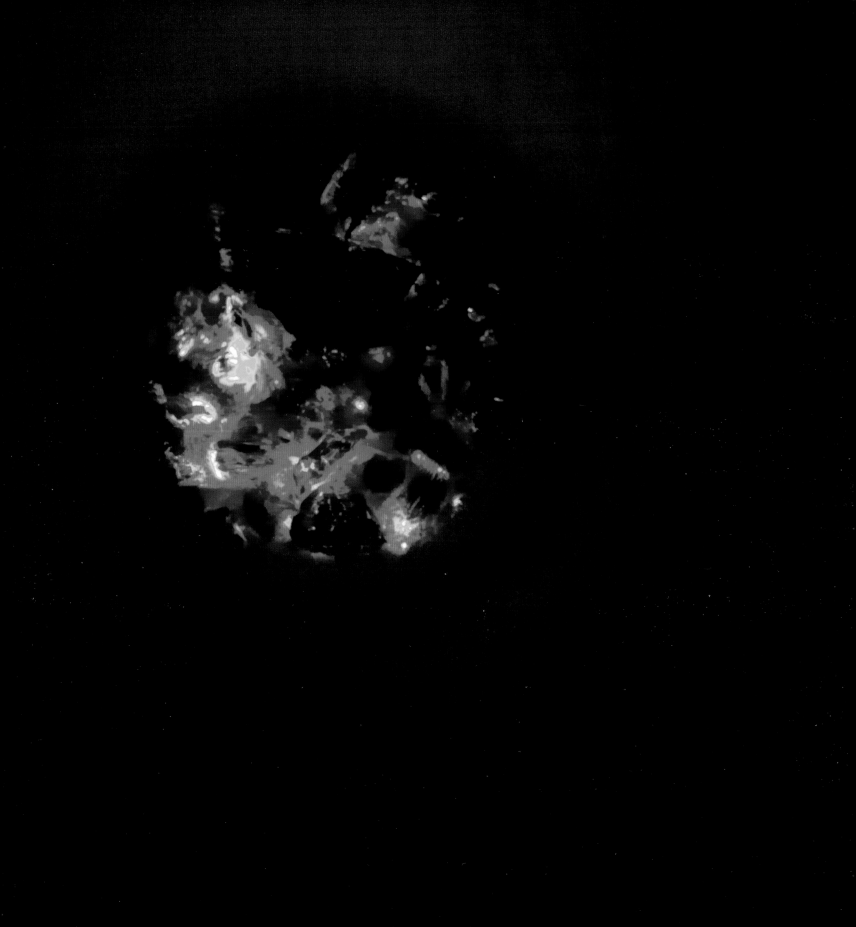

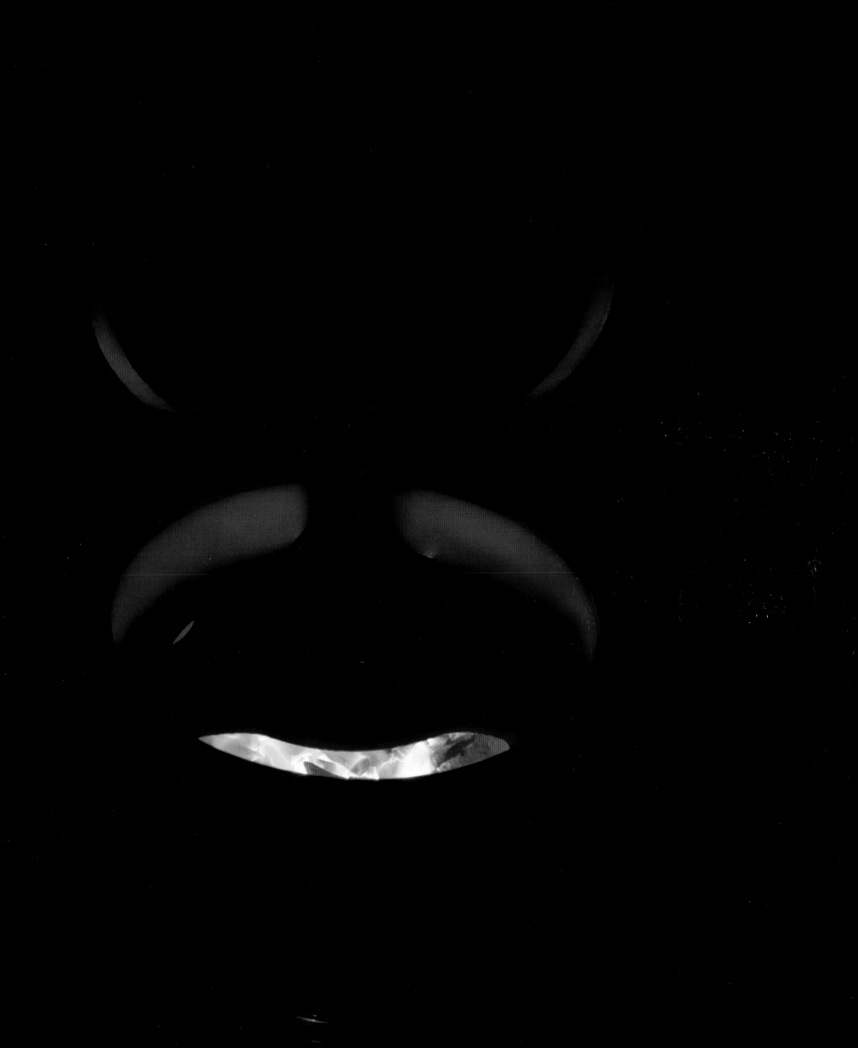

THE BIG GREEN EGG® BOOK

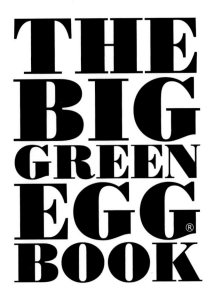

THE BIG GREEN EGG BOOK

edited by **DIRK KOPPES**

recipes by **VANJA VAN DER LEEDEN**

photography by **REMKO KRAAIJEVELD**

design by **RONALD TIMMERMANS**

Andrews McMeel
Publishing®

Kansas City • Sydney • London

Big
Green
Egg

CONTENTS

TIME
FOR A NEW
TRADITION

Twenty years ago, I dug a hole in the ground, filled it with wood chips, and lit a fire. I threw in some wild mint, followed by a suckling pig, and covered the pit with sod. The glowing embers burned all night, and the next day friends came over to eat the roasted pig. They had never eaten pig cooked that way. Yet this method couldn't have been simpler.

Grilling is the epitome of slow cooking, but some people are more inclined to buy a cheap grill, add charcoal and starter fluid, and cook their first pork chops. What they will end up with is a petroleum taste and a poor-quality product. There is a better way.

Time for a new tradition!

About ten years ago, I discovered the Big Green Egg. It was love at first sight, and I had to have one. I am a gadget man at heart, but the appliance must serve a purpose. There is only so much room at my restaurant, De Librije, so I am selective about my cooking equipment. It was an easy decision to make room for the Big Green Egg.

De Librije was one of the first restaurants in the Netherlands with an EGG, and we have now been serving dishes cooked in it for over ten years. The best thing about the EGG is that it cooks foods very evenly, especially when you close the lid. Fish and particularly meat can be cooked until it falls off the bone. The Big Green Egg is a grill and oven rolled into one.

The moment the grill arrived, we started it up right away with birch wood chips in flames filling the dome. In no time, the wood chips were reduced to embers, and we were ready to cook. We had breakfast next to the EGG, which seemed similar to an open-pit fireplace. At that time, I was experimenting with wood chips and gale, a species of flowering plant that grows locally and is used in beer making.

The taste of gale is quite bitter, but the aroma is delicious. When you grill with a mixture of wood chips and gale, you get a heavy cinnamon-like fragrance. If you grill sweetbreads, they will turn out delightful. We still cook sweetbreads this way, but with juniper berries in place of the gale. The Big Green Egg is mobile, so every once in a while we take it out to the restaurant patio and serve mini pizzas with an aperitif. You start by placing pizza dough rounds on the grill. The high heat cooks the pizzas quickly, which makes the dough crispy on the outside and tender on the inside. They are great for a quick bite.

When I owned a boat, every Sunday my wife, Thérèse, the kids, and I would go sailing while the EGG was cooking. We would fire it up in the morning and four hours later we would be eating lobster or fish. When I am enjoying downtime with my family, I really go all out with the EGG.

It is time for the Big Green Egg! You can have so much fun with it. Don't stash it away in the closet. Instead, experiment and use it as an oven. You can add flavor to vegetables, fruits, or even chocolate. Or, add variety through different-flavored wood chips (see page 196) or equipment. The key is to be creative. Sometimes it takes only a minute for the flavor you desire and other times it will take much longer. Throw on some sweet potatoes or eggplant and see what happens—brilliant!

I don't want to become the poster boy for a new tradition, but I do hope this book will inspire you to try the recipes my colleagues and I have been enjoying over the years. I wish you many culinary adventures.

Jonnie Boer, Restaurant De Librije

THE CULINARY FUTURE

The origins of the Big Green Egg actually go back two millennia. Originating from cookers that were not much more than clay vessels with lids, today's EGG is a modern ceramic marvel known for producing amazing, unique flavors and culinary results that inspire both home cooks and chefs at three-star restaurants, all looking for new ways to create great food.

Cooking outside on an open fire awakens our primal instincts. As a species, our survival is dependent on finding sources of food. The writer James Boswell described man as "a cooking animal. The beasts have memory, judgment, and all the faculties and passions of our mind, in a certain degree; but no beast is a cook." We benefit from cooking with fire because we can consume different varieties of seeds and roots without having to chew on them all day like cows do. This saves us valuable time to pursue other fun things.

Scholars differ over the exact time period humans started cooking and learned to master fire. Sigmund Freud thought we reached our aha moment when man overcame his insistence on putting out brush fires by urinating on them. Then, voilà, *the* fire, and cooking became an important element of how we prepare our food.

The Greeks saw Prometheus as the founder of the first cooking method used by humans: he defied the gods and stole the fire for mankind. The Chinese have their own version of grilling dating back thousands of years to the use of egg-shaped clay bowls for preparing food. Those little bowls would be transformed into egg-shaped cookers.

Origin

The first large clay cookers in China appeared during the Qin dynasty (221 to 206 BCE). The Japanese spent the next three centuries coming up with the kamado (a Japanese word meaning stove or cooking place), which was similar to an oven or fireplace. In time, people adapted these units so that the food cooked on a grid above a fire pit and moved them into kitchen-like areas, where they were used for grilling and roasting meat.

Over the centuries, the kamado took on various forms: one for the kitchen, a portable version for traveling (the first real grill), and a mushi-kamado for cooking rice. Many Japanese used at least two of these units for cooking.

After World War II, American troops learned how to cook with the kamado from the Japanese. They discovered that it retained heat and moisture better than a standard grill and turned out better tasting, more aromatic dishes, so when it was time to return home, they brought the kamado back to the States.

Invention

Navy Lieutenant Ed Fisher first came across the kamado in Japan during the 1950s. Although he wasn't quite sure what to do with it, he did notice that whenever he prepared chicken in it, the neighbors wanted to come over for dinner. In 1974, when Fisher opened the Pachinko House in Atlanta, Georgia, he sold pinball machines and an assortment of kamados. Business was not great, and the kamados collected dust on a back shelf. Customers were allowed to take a kamado home to try it out, but they typically returned it, complaining that it cracked or broke apart.

Fisher decided to keep the original shape (an enclosed space that retains heat and smoke) of the kamado, but he knew that what it was made of needed a twentieth-century makeover. So, he changed the materials radically: no clay or inexpensive metal. Fisher made exploratory trips to ceramic factories and eventually found a heavy-duty, insulating ceramic material. It was nearly indestructible, resistant to wind and rain, impervious to extreme temperatures, and user-friendly. No tears or cracks appeared after prolonged use—the ideal solution.

Design
You can have a good-quality product, but you still need to sell it to the customer. Fisher chose a striking green for the color and combined the shape with the name, the Big Green Egg. It was sturdy, yet attractive enough to catch the eye. Fisher was the first to install a thermometer in the lid, which made it easy both to check and to control the temperature while cooking. The grill also converted into an outdoor oven.

Because there wasn't much money for an advertising budget, Fisher relied on word of mouth to promote the Big Green Egg. One enthusiastic EGG user led to more, and soon there was a big following. These enthusiasts called themselves EGGheads and organized EGGfests.

The EGG has been used by chefs in the Netherlands and Belgium for more than a decade. It was love at first sight for Jonnie Boer, Sergio Herman, Lucas Rive (a barbecue world champion), columnist Wim de Jong from the Dutch newspaper *Volkskrant*, and Golden Earring drummer Cesar Zuiderwijk. Shopkeeper Marc van Steenbeek, who sells professional kitchen equipment, has called the EGG "the most beautiful culinary barbecue." Sergio Herman said, "Wow! I was sold right away. This was more than a grill. This is a smart culinary tool that I had never seen before. It was a grill, smoker, and oven all in one—and the temperature can be carefully controlled. I thought right away that I could really do something with this in the kitchen." Wim de Jong wanted to get back to basics and bought an EGG in 2008. He was especially taken with its durability and simplicity, saying, "People who enjoy cooking will be equally pleased."

Superiority
What is the value of a Big Green Egg? Forget the traditional grill with charcoal-cooked steaks that are raw inside. With the EGG, anyone can cook succulent steaks or fish. The airflow can be adjusted from the top or the bottom, allowing pizzas to be cooked at 660°F (350°C) and slower cooking foods at 200°F (93°C). For example, to achieve crusty toppings,

simply adjust the dial to a higher setting. The temperature can reach as high as 750°F (400°C), much like an infrared grill, but the EGG can also maintain a low temperature like an old-fashioned grill that uses flavored wood chips. Sprigs of rosemary can add extra flavor to homemade pizza (or to smoked lamb, the way Jonnie Boer prepares it).

A standard grill works satisfactorily if all you want to do is grill your food. But if you want to smoke fish, for example, or simply add extra flavor, then the Big Green Egg is for you.

The thick ceramic walls isolate and hold the heat inside, yet the outside stays cool to the touch. The ancient design, with modern materials, circulates the heat inside the EGG and helps to control the temperature. The dome-like lid stays closed during the cooking process so that heat comes from above, not just from the charcoal below. More important, the tight-fitting lid ensures that the food retains moisture—the natural flavors and juices are preserved, lessening the shrinking that typically occurs when food cooks. Constantly turning skewers is a thing of the past with the Big Green Egg. The heat inside the dome is evenly distributed, eliminating the need to rotate food continually to achieve uniform cooking.

Chefs insist on charcoal, not briquettes, for the EGG. Briquettes can give off chemical odors and affect taste. Charcoal lights faster, is easier to use, and while charcoal is more expensive, the cost is cheaper overall because charcoal lasts longer. In 2012, the chefs from Amsterdam's Smokey Goodness set an official Guinness World Record when they cooked for fifty-two continuous hours with the Big Green Egg.

Food guru Michael Pollan explains the attraction of the EGG as our craving for "real cooking." He continues, "We spend more time looking at cooking shows than actually cooking. That has to change. We need and must do the work ourselves. With fresh ingredients you want to prepare your own food. And isn't a barbecue much more fun than a microwave? It's all about the four elements, especially fire, and what you do with it." Pollan believes the shape of the Big Green Egg is superior at controlling burning.

You don't need prepackaged food to use the EGG. Grab some meat and let it cook for several hours. Phenomenal.

Dirk Koppes

LET'S GET TO WORK WITH THE BIG GREEN EGG

SERVES 6	COOKING TIME	GRILL TEMPERATURE	EQUIPMENT
	10 to 12 minutes	Set the EGG for direct cooking	Cast Iron Grid
	(+ 10 minutes to marinate)	with the Cast Iron Grid.	
		Preheat the EGG to 350°F (180°C).	

The best-tasting eggplant has been cooked until tender and caramel-like. To prepare it perfectly, cook as directed here, then allow the steaks to marinate in the dressing for 10 minutes before serving. This dish is delicious served with a watercress salad and raw or grilled zucchini strips with capers.

EGGPLANT STEAKS
with fennel-rosemary dressing and buffalo mozzarella

Ingredients

FENNEL-ROSEMARY DRESSING
2 cloves garlic
1 teaspoon coarse sea salt
2 teaspoons fennel seeds
2 red bell peppers, seeded and finely chopped
Leaves from 9 rosemary sprigs, very finely chopped
⅓ cup (75 ml) extra-virgin olive oil

EGGPLANT
3 medium eggplants
Olive oil, for rubbing
Salt and freshly ground black pepper
1 lemon, halved
Buffalo mozzarella cheese, broken into small pieces, for garnish
Oil-packed anchovy fillets, for garnish
Leaves from 3 mint sprigs, for garnish

Preparation

FENNEL-ROSEMARY DRESSING
With a mortar and pestle, mash together the garlic, salt, and fennel seeds until a paste forms. Transfer to a small bowl, add the bell peppers, rosemary, and oil, and mix well. Set aside.

EGGPLANT
Cut each eggplant lengthwise into slices ¼ inch (6 mm) thick. Rub both sides of each slice with oil and then sprinkle with salt and pepper. Place the slices on the Cast Iron Grid, close the lid of the EGG, and grill for 5 to 6 minutes on each side, until tender. Grill the lemon halves alongside the eggplant for 1 to 2 minutes, until lightly charred.

Arrange the eggplant steaks on a platter. Squeeze the juice from the lemon into the reserved dressing, then rub the steaks with the lemon halves. Pour the dressing over the steaks and let stand for 10 minutes.

TO FINISH
Scatter the cheese, anchovy fillets, and mint leaves over the eggplant steaks.

GRILL TEMPERATURE

Set the EGG for direct cooking.

Preheat the EGG to just below 475°F (250°C).

COOKING TIME

3 to 4 minutes

SERVES 6

OYSTERS IN THEIR OWN JUICES

with clarified citrus butter and mescal

These oysters take flavor to a new level! Oysters absorb their own juices when cooked in the shell, which enhances their flavor and makes their shells easier to open. A successful formula! Be careful not to overcook the oysters. They should still be a bit raw when served.

Ingredients

CLARIFIED BUTTER

1 cup plus 2 tablespoons (250 g) unsalted butter

Grated zest of ½ lemon

Fleur de sel

OYSTERS

24 oysters in the shells

Dash of mescal or peat-flavored Scotch whisky, for each oyster

2 chives, finely chopped

Grated fresh horseradish root, for garnish

Preparation

CLARIFIED BUTTER

Melt the butter in a saucepan on the stove top over medium-low heat, skimming off any foam as it forms on the surface and allowing the solids to settle to the bottom of the pan. Pour the clear golden butter through a fine-mesh sieve into a heatproof bowl. Discard the solids at the bottom of the pan. Season the butter with the lemon zest and salt. Return the butter to the saucepan and keep warm until needed.

OYSTERS

Place the oysters, with the more deeply curved half shell facing upward, on the cooking grid. Close the lid of the EGG and let cook for 3 to 4 minutes, just until the shells crack open and release a little steam. Transfer the oysters to a platter.

Using an oyster knife or paring knife, pry off the top shell from each oyster. Slide the knife under each oyster meat to sever the muscle that attaches it to the bottom shell, and leave the oyster in the shell. Discard any oysters that failed to open.

TO FINISH

Top each oyster with a little clarified butter and a dash of mescal, then sprinkle with the chives and with horseradish to taste.

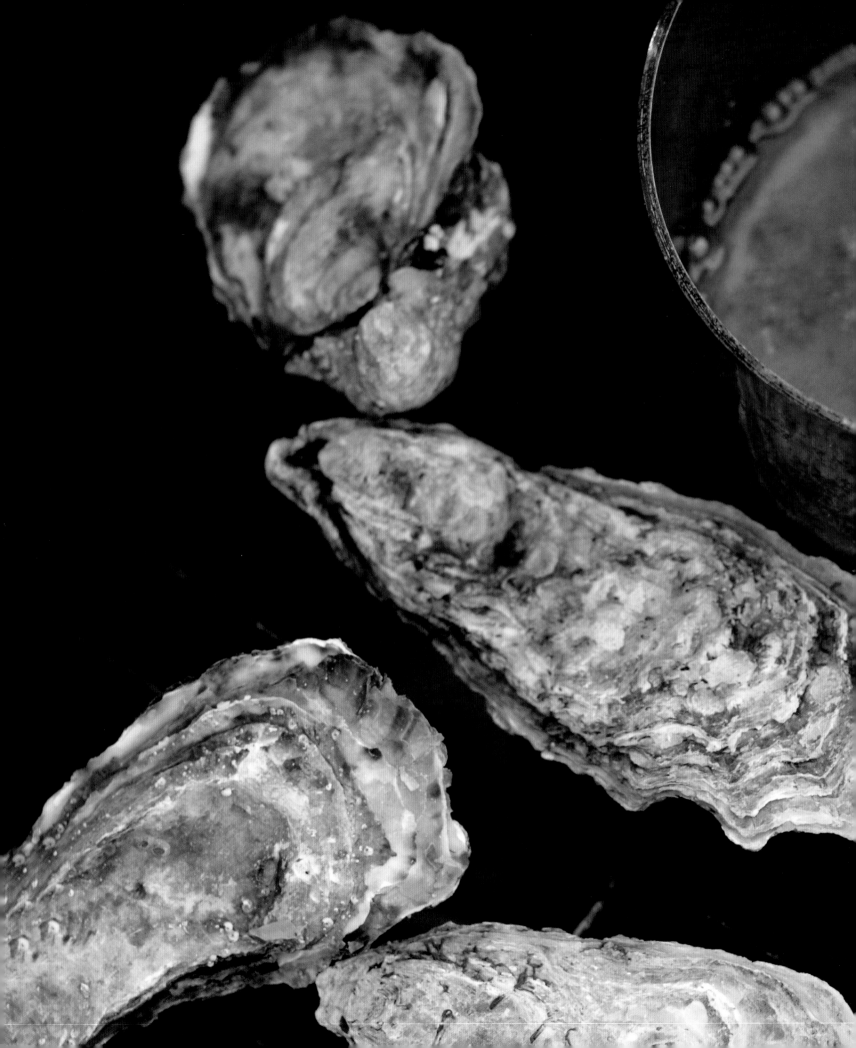

EQUIPMENT	GRILL TEMPERATURE	COOKING TIME	SERVES 6
convEGGtor	Set the EGG for indirect cooking.	5 minutes	
Round Grill Wok	Preheat the EGG to 475°F (240°C).	(+ 45 minutes to cook the rice)	

RAZOR CLAMS AND BABY CLAMS

with chermoula and risotto made from black rice

In this recipe, banana leaves lend a wonderful fragrance to the shellfish. If you do not have a Round Grill Wok, you can lace the banana leaves together with small skewers to create a cooking vessel.

Ingredients

BLACK RICE
8 cups (2 L) water
1 kohlrabi, trimmed and cut into matchsticks
Juice of 1 orange
Salt and freshly ground black pepper
1 tablespoon olive oil
1 shallot, diced
Few fresh bay leaves
2¾ cups (500 g) black rice, rinsed
½ cup (120 ml) white wine

CHERMOULA
Pinch of saffron threads
1 teaspoon water, lukewarm
2 cloves garlic
1 teaspoon coarse sea salt
1 red bell pepper, seeded and finely chopped
2 tablespoons caraway seeds
Juice of 1 lemon
1 bunch cilantro, coarsely chopped
½ cup (120 ml) olive oil
Salt

RAZOR CLAMS AND BABY CLAMS
1⅔ pounds (750 g) cockles or small clams
1⅔ pounds (750 g) mussels
1⅔ pounds (750 g) razor clams
Banana leaves, soaked in water to soften
¼ cup (60 ml) white wine
Salt and freshly ground black pepper

Preparation

BLACK RICE
Bring the water to a simmer in a saucepan over high heat on the stove top, then turn down the heat to the lowest setting. While the water is heating, in a bowl, combine the kohlrabi, orange juice, and a pinch of salt and set aside to marinate.

Heat the oil in a large saucepan over medium heat on the stove top. Add the shallot and bay leaves and cook, stirring often, for 2 to 3 minutes, until the shallot is soft. Add the rice and cook, stirring often, for 1 to 2 minutes. Turn down the heat to medium-low, pour in the wine, and cook, stirring, until it is absorbed. Add a ladleful of the hot water and cook, stirring constantly, until the liquid is almost fully absorbed. Add another ladleful of water and again cook, stirring, until the rice is almost dry. Continue to add the water in this manner for 35 to 40 minutes, until the rice is tender but still slightly chewy. About 10 minutes before the rice is ready, stir in the kohlrabi mixture. When the rice is done, taste and adjust the seasoning with salt and pepper.

CHERMOULA
Soak the saffron threads in the water and set aside. With a mortar and pestle, mash together the garlic and sea salt to form a paste. Add the bell pepper, caraway seeds, the saffron and water, and lemon juice and continue to mash. Transfer the mixture to a small bowl, add the cilantro and oil, and mix well. Season with salt.

RAZOR CLAMS AND BABY CLAMS
Rinse the cockles and mussels thoroughly to remove any sand. Rinse the razor clams under running water. Line the Round Grill Wok with a generous layer of banana leaves to keep the juices contained. Place the cockles, mussels, and razor clams on the leaves. Place the Wok on the cooking grid, close the lid of the EGG, and cook for 3 to 4 minutes. Add the wine, close the lid of the EGG, and continue cooking until most of the liquid evaporates. Season with salt and pepper. Discard any shellfish that failed to open.

TO FINISH
Serve the shellfish on the banana leaves with the black rice on the side. Garnish with the chermoula.

MAKES 6 PIZZAS	COOKING TIME	GRILL TEMPERATURE	EQUIPMENT
	5 to 7 minutes per pizza (+ 1½ hours for the dough to rise and 10 to 12 minutes to cook the sauce)	Set the EGG for indirect cooking with the Pizza & Baking Stone on the grid. Preheat the EGG to 570° to 700°F (300° to 375°C).	convEGGtor Pizza & Baking Stone Dough Rolling Mat or flat work surface Pizza Peel or rimless baking sheet

A pizza grilled at the correct temperature in the Big Green Egg tastes like a pizza baked in a wood-fired oven. Here, a trio of classic toppings—buffalo mozzarella, aromatic basil, ripe tomatoes—is arranged on homemade dough, a combination that promises to become one of your favorite pizzas.

PIZZA QUATTRO COLORI
with tomatoes and basil

Ingredients

PIZZA DOUGH
3 tablespoons crumbled fresh yeast (1⅓ ounces/35 g)
2 tablespoons sugar
2¾ cups (650 ml) water, lukewarm (90° to 100°F/32° to 38°C)
¼ cup (60 ml) olive oil
8 cups (1 kg) 00 flour or all-purpose flour
1 tablespoon fine sea salt
Cornmeal, for dusting

TOPPING
1 (28-ounce/800-g) can whole tomatoes, drained and cut into chunks
Salt and freshly ground black pepper
1 pound (500 g) assorted fresh tomatoes (such as yellow, beefsteak, cherry or grape, San Marzano, and/or heirloom varieties)
1½ pounds (680 g) buffalo mozzarella cheese
1 (2-ounce/55-g) can oil-packed anchovy fillets, drained
Leaves from 1 small bunch purple basil
Leaves from 1 small bunch green basil
Olive oil or chili oil, for drizzling

Preparation

PIZZA DOUGH
In a medium bowl, mix the yeast and sugar into the water, stirring until dissolved. Stir in the oil and set aside for 5 to 10 minutes, until foamy. Sift the flour with the salt into a mound on a clean, flat work surface or into a large bowl. Form a small well in the center of the mound and pour the reserved yeast-sugar mixture into the well. Using a wooden spoon, slowly work the flour mixture into the yeast mixture. When the mixture is too heavy to work with a spoon, switch to your hands and knead until a supple dough forms. Coat a large bowl with flour and transfer the dough to the bowl. Cover the bowl with a damp kitchen towel and let the dough rise in a warm place for about 1½ hours, or until doubled in size. Just before using, turn out the dough onto a lightly floured surface and knead several times to remove any air bubbles.

TOPPING
Place the canned tomatoes in a sauté pan over medium heat on the stove top. Season with salt and pepper and cook, stirring occasionally, for 10 to 12 minutes, until the tomatoes break down and form a thick, chunky sauce. Set aside.

Cut the fresh tomatoes into slices or halve the smaller ones and set aside. Break the mozzarella into pieces and set aside.

BAKING
Divide the dough into 6 equal portions and flatten each portion into a disk. Place a disk on the Dough Rolling Mat or a lightly floured work surface and, using a floured rolling pin, roll out into a circle about ¼ inch (6 mm) thick. Dust the Pizza Peel or sheet pan with cornmeal and transfer the dough circle to the Peel. Spread the dough circle evenly with one-sixth of the tomato sauce and top with one-sixth each of the fresh tomatoes and mozzarella pieces. Gently shake the Peel to make sure the dough is not sticking to it. Slide the pizza onto the preheated Pizza & Baking Stone. Close the lid of the EGG and bake for 5 to 7 minutes, until the edges are crisp and brown.

TO FINISH
Using the Peel, remove the pizza from the EGG and top with one-sixth each of the anchovies and basil. Drizzle with oil and serve immediately. Repeat with the remaining dough and toppings.

EQUIPMENT
2 flexible skewers or long
metal skewers

GRILL TEMPERATURE
Set the EGG for direct cooking.
Preheat the EGG to 200°F (100°C).

COOKING TIME
30 minutes

SERVES 6

BLACKENED VEGETABLES with tzatziki

Using coals left over from grilling something else works well for this dish, because the coals remain just hot enough for direct contact with the vegetables. The outside leaves of the artichokes will be somewhat charred and should be discarded, but the inside leaves will have a wonderful smoky flavor.

Ingredients

BLACKENED VEGETABLES
12 small artichokes
Olive oil, for drizzling and rubbing
Fine sea salt, for sprinkling
6 green bell peppers

TZATZIKI
1 cucumber
1 teaspoon fine sea salt
1 clove garlic
1 teaspoon coarse sea salt
1½ cups (300 g) plain Greek yogurt
Grated zest of 1 lemon
1 bunch dill, finely chopped
Few fresh mint leaves
Dash of fruity olive oil (such as Tuscan)
Pinch of black sesame seeds, for garnish
(optional)

TO FINISH
1 lemon, halved
Salt and freshly ground black pepper
Grated or shaved Parmesan cheese,
for sprinkling

Preparation

BLACKENED VEGETABLES
Trim the stem end of each artichoke, then turn the artichokes upside down and apply light pressure to separate the leaves slightly. This will create improved air circulation around the leaves. Drizzle the leaves with oil and sprinkle with salt. Place the artichokes, stem end down, on the hot coals, close the lid of the EGG, and cook for about 30 minutes, or until the outer leaves are charred and the bottom is easily pierced with a skewer.

Meanwhile, thread the bell peppers onto the skewers and sprinkle with salt. Rub the bell peppers with some oil. Place the peppers on the coals alongside the artichokes, close the lid of the EGG, and cook, turning the bell peppers every 5 minutes, for a total of 10 to 15 minutes, until charred in spots and softened.

TZATZIKI
Cut the cucumber lengthwise into quarters. Trim away the seeds from each quarter. Place a fine-mesh sieve over a bowl. Using the large holes on a handheld grater, coarsely grate the cucumber over the sieve. Sprinkle the cucumber with the fine sea salt and leave to drain.

With a mortar and pestle, mash together the garlic and coarse sea salt until a paste forms. Spoon the yogurt into a bowl, add the garlic paste and lemon zest, mix well, and stir in the dill and cucumber. Garnish with the mint and oil and sprinkle with the black sesame seeds.

TO FINISH
Spread the outside leaves of the artichokes and cut each artichoke in half lengthwise. Squeeze the lemon halves over the artichokes and sprinkle with salt, pepper, and Parmesan. Serve with the blackened bell peppers and tzatziki.

EQUIPMENT

Handful of wood chips, soaked in water
for at least 30 minutes
Cast Iron Grid
Half Moon Cast Iron Griddle (smooth side)

GRILL TEMPERATURE

Set the EGG for direct cooking without the grid.
Preheat the EGG to 390°F (200°C), then lower
to 350°F (180°C).

COOKING TIME

16 to 18 minutes
(+ 3 minutes to cook the egg yolks)

SERVES 6

SMOKY BURGER

with miso butter, kimchi, and fried egg yolk

Chuck from the shoulder is used in this recipe, as it has just enough fat to keep the burgers juicy. There are many other meat options for making burgers, but the choice should always be fresh and lean, and it must never be ground more than twice to ensure the correct consistency. A piece of miso butter slipped into the center of each patty helps the burgers to retain their moisture and gives them a unique flavor.

Ingredients

MISO BUTTER
5 tablespoons (85 g) white miso
⅓ cup (75 g) unsalted butter, at room temperature
1 tablespoon sherry vinegar
1 tablespoon cayenne pepper

HAMBURGERS
2½ pounds (1.2 kg) ground chuck
Salt and freshly ground black pepper
6 tomatoes, halved crosswise
6 egg yolks
Canola oil, for frying
6 good-quality hamburger buns, split
6 lettuce leaves
Kimchi, for topping
Fleur de sel
Watercress sprouts, for garnish

Preparation

MISO BUTTER
In a small bowl, combine the miso, butter, vinegar, and cayenne pepper and mix well. Set aside in a cool place.

HAMBURGERS
Season the meat with salt and pepper, then divide into 6 equal portions. Shape each portion into a thick patty. Shape the miso butter into 6 small disks (each about 1 inch/2.5 cm in diameter) and slip a disk into the center of each patty. Make sure the miso butter is securely enclosed within the center of each patty so it will not leak out. Reserve the remaining butter.

Scatter the soaked wood chips over the hot coals, place the Cast Iron Grid and the Half Moon Cast Iron Griddle (smooth side up) in the EGG, and close the lid of the EGG to preheat the Grid and Griddle. Place the patties on the preheated Grid, close the lid of the EGG, and cook for 3 to 4 minutes on each side. Move the burgers to the Griddle, close the lid of the EGG, and cook for 10 minutes. Sprinkle the tomato halves with salt and pepper, place them cut side up on the Grid, close the lid, and cook alongside the burgers for 3 to 4 minutes, until softened.

TO FINISH
Pour just enough oil into a frying pan to film the bottom and place the pan over medium heat on the stove top. Add the egg yolks and cook for a few minutes, just until the bottoms of the yolks have solidified and the tops are still soft. Carefully remove the yolks from the pan.

Spread the remaining miso butter on the cut sides of the buns. Place a lettuce leaf on each bun bottom and top with kimchi, 2 tomato halves, and a burger. Finish off with a fried egg yolk, season with fleur de sel, and garnish with watercress sprouts.

COOKING TIME

5 to 6 minutes

(+ 1 to 2 hours to marinate)

GRILL TEMPERATURE

Set the EGG for direct cooking with the Perforated Cooking Grid. Preheat the EGG to 390°F (200°C).

EQUIPMENT

Perforated Cooking Grid (round)

The trick to preparing flavorful prawns is to peel them so that the marinade is in direct contact with the meat. The banana leaves serve a dual purpose here: they prevent the sherry from escaping into the coals and they create an attractive presentation. These prawns make a great appetizer with a glass of dry sherry.

TIGER PRAWNS
with sherry and black vinegar

Ingredients

PRAWNS

2¼ pounds (1 kg) prawns in the shell

2 cloves garlic

1 teaspoon coarse sea salt

1 red bell pepper, seeded and diced

2 tablespoons Chinese black vinegar

Scant ½ cup (100 ml) soy sauce

Dash of Asian sesame oil

2 banana leaves, soaked in water to soften

Large dash of medium sherry

1 lemon, cut into wedges, for garnish

Finely minced fresh cilantro, for garnish

Preparation

PRAWNS

Peel and devein the prawns, keeping the heads and the tails segments intact. With a mortar and pestle, mash together the garlic and salt until a paste forms. Transfer the paste to a large bowl, add the bell pepper, vinegar, soy sauce, and sesame oil, and mix well. Add the prawns and turn to coat evenly with the marinade. Cover and let stand at room temperature for 1 to 2 hours.

TO FINISH

Lay the banana leaves atop each other to form a cross. This will make them easier to pick up and move to the EGG. Remove the prawns from the marinade and place atop the banana leaves in a single layer. Transfer the leaves with the prawns to the Perforated Cooking Grid, close the lid of the EGG, and cook for 2½ to 3 minutes on each side, until they turn pink. Add the sherry, remove from the EGG, and serve the prawns in the banana leaves, garnished with the lemon wedges and cilantro.

Chef's Flavor Injector
convEGGtor
Roasting & Drip Pan
Meat thermometer
Meat claws or 2 forks

Set the EGG for indirect cooking.
Preheat the EGG to 200°F (100°C).

6 to 7 hours
(+ overnight to marinate)

PULLED PORK
with coleslaw and cilantro mayonnaise

Have you been bombarded with talk of pulled pork? From cooking shows to the chef's specialty section on many menus, this old-fashioned dish seems to be everywhere. It takes about seven hours of slow cooking before the meat will pull easily from the bone, so is the taste worth the wait? Yes, because if cooked properly, pulled pork is delicious.

Ingredients

Preparation

MARINADE

3 cloves garlic
1 small piece fresh ginger, peeled
1 cup (240 ml) apple cider
¼ cup (60 ml) cider vinegar
1 teaspoon Tabasco sauce
2 tablespoons Worcestershire sauce
3 tablespoons soy sauce
1 teaspoon freshly grated nutmeg
1 teaspoon ground cinnamon

RUB

2 tablespoons cayenne pepper
2 tablespoons sweet paprika
2 tablespoons dark brown sugar
2 tablespoons fine sea salt

PULLED PORK

1 (5½-pound/2.5 kg) bone-in pork shoulder

COLESLAW

2 tablespoons cumin seeds
2 teaspoons granulated sugar
2 teaspoons salt
2 tablespoons red wine vinegar
½ head red cabbage, finely shredded
1 carrot, peeled and julienned
2 small red bell peppers, seeded and finely chopped

CILANTRO MAYONNAISE

2 egg yolks, at room temperature
3½ tablespoons fresh lemon juice
Salt and freshly ground black pepper
2 cups (480 ml) sunflower oil
Chopped fresh cilantro, for seasoning

6 rolls, partially split lengthwise

MARINADE

Using a fine-rasp grater held over a medium bowl, grate the garlic and ginger into a pulp. Add the cider, vinegar, Tabasco sauce, Worcestershire sauce, soy sauce, nutmeg, and cinnamon and mix well. Transfer the marinade to the Chef's Flavor Injector and inject the marinade into the pork.

RUB

In a small bowl, combine all the ingredients, mixing well. Rub the pork evenly with the rub. Place the pork in a large resealable plastic bag, seal the bag closed, and refrigerate overnight.

PULLED PORK

Carefully build the fire, placing large pieces of natural lump charcoal underneath the fire box up to the rim. Make sure the vents are not blocked. Allow the fire to burn for at least 7 hours before grilling.

Place the convEGGtor, with the legs facing up, in the EGG. Pour a small amount of water into the Roasting & Drip Pan, then place the Roasting & Drip Pan on the convEGGtor. Use the juices and fat drippings that collect in the Roasting & Drip Pan to baste the pork occasionally as it cooks. Place the cooking grid on the convEGGtor. Insert the meat thermometer into the pork away from bone, place the pork on the cooking grid, and close the lid of the EGG. The temperature of the meat should hover around 155°F (70°C) for about 6 hours. After 6 hours, wrap the meat in aluminum foil,

return it to the grid, close the lid of the EGG, and cook until the temperature rises to 175°F (80°C). If needed, raise the temperature of the EGG to 285°F (140°C) to ensure the meat is properly cooked.

COLESLAW

In a small, dry frying pan, toast the cumin seeds over medium heat on the stove top, shaking the pan often, for a few minutes, or until fragrant. Pour onto a small plate and let cool. In a large bowl, combine the granulated sugar, salt, and vinegar and stir until the sugar and salt dissolve. Add the cabbage, carrot, and bell peppers and toss to coat evenly with the dressing. Add the cumin seeds and toss to mix.

CILANTRO MAYO

In a blender, combine the egg yolks, lemon juice, and a pinch each of salt and pepper and process on low speed until well blended. With the blender running continuously, add the oil in a very fine, slow stream and process until the mixture is thick and smooth. (Once an emulsion has formed, the oil can be added a little more quickly.) Transfer the mayonnaise to a small bowl and stir in the cilantro to taste. This makes quite a bit of mayo, but because it is delicious, that's okay! Store the leftover in a tightly covered container in the refrigerator for up to 1 week.

TO FINISH

Using the meat claws or 2 forks, pull the pork off of the bone in long shreds. Spread the cut sides of each roll with the mayo. Add the coleslaw to the rolls and top generously with the pulled pork.

SERVES 6	COOKING TIME	GRILL TEMPERATURE	EQUIPMENT
	12 minutes	Set the EGG for direct cooking with	Half Moon Cast Iron Griddle (smooth side)
	(+ 10 minutes to "cook" the couscous)	the Half Moon Cast Iron Griddle.	Perforated Cooking Grid (round or square)
		Preheat the EGG to 350°F (180°C).	

This main course is a variation of *sarde a beccafico*, the Sicilian classic. The *beccafico* is a bird that feeds only on ripe figs, creating a very rich, tasty meat. This recipe is made with a mixture of pine nuts, anchovies, raisins, and cinnamon—ingredients reminiscent of baroque Sicily. Fill the sardines with a portion of the seasoned couscous, and serve the grilled fish on the remaining couscous.

SICILIAN SARDINES
filled with couscous

Ingredients

SARDINES
3⅓ pounds (1.5 kg) sardines
Juice of 2 oranges
Olive oil, for rubbing

COUSCOUS
2⅓ cups (400 g) quick-cooking couscous
Boiling water, to cover
6 tablespoons (90 ml) olive oil
Pinch of salt
4 tablespoons almonds
4 tablespoons pine nuts
5 ounces (150 g) young fava beans in the pod, shelled
8 oil-packed anchovy fillets, coarsely chopped
3 tablespoons raisins, plumped in Marsala or sherry, drained, and coarsely chopped
1 small bunch flat-leaf parsley, coarsely chopped
2 strips candied lemon peel, very finely chopped
Juice of 1 lemon
1 teaspoon ground cinnamon
Salt and freshly ground black pepper

Preparation

SARDINES
Clean and scale the sardines, then butterfly each fish by carefully slicing open the belly and removing the spine and rib cage. Rinse under cold running water, pat dry, and place in a shallow bowl. Add the orange juice and turn the fish to coat evenly.

COUSCOUS/FILLING
Put the couscous in a heatproof bowl and add the boiling water nearly to cover. Add 2 tablespoons of the oil and the salt, cover, and let stand for 10 minutes. Then, using a fork, fluff the couscous with a fork.

Place the almonds and pine nuts on the Half Moon Cast Iron Griddle, smooth side up, close the lid of EGG, and cook, stirring and checking occasionally, until toasted. This will take only a few minutes.

Bring a small saucepan filled with water to a boil on the stove top. Add the fava beans and boil for 3 minutes. Drain, let cool, then remove their outer skins.

Add the nuts, fava beans, anchovies, raisins, parsley, and candied lemon peel to the couscous and stir and toss to mix. Add the remaining 4 tablespoons (60 ml) olive oil and the lemon juice and mix well. Add the cinnamon and season with salt and pepper.

TO FINISH
Carefully remove the Griddle from the grid and replace with the Perforated Cooking Grid. Remove the sardines from the orange juice and pat dry. Stuff each sardine with some of the couscous and secure the opening closed with a skewer. Rub the sardines with oil. Place the sardines on the Grid, close the lid of the EGG, and grill for 5 to 6 minutes, until done. Serve the sardines on top of the remaining couscous.

EQUIPMENT

Small ovenproof frying pan
Perforated Cooking Grid (round)

GRILL TEMPERATURE

Set the EGG for direct cooking.
Preheat the EGG to 350°F (180°C).

COOKING TIME

20 minutes

SERVES 6

SPICY CHICKEN LIVERS
with grilled yellow bell peppers and cilantro

Concerned your dinner guests are not adventurous enough for chicken livers? No worries, this spicy dish will win them over. Serve as an appetizer with crusty bread.

Ingredients

SALAD

3 yellow bell peppers
⅓ cup (50 g) blanched hazelnuts

CHICKEN LIVERS

1 pound (450 g) organic chicken livers
2 cloves garlic, minced
2 tablespoons red pepper flakes
Pinch of saffron threads, soaked in
1 tablespoon water
Olive oil, for frying
Dash of orange blossom water
Dash of Cognac
Fleur de sel
1 teaspoon lavender salt
Juice of 1 lemon
Mixed salad greens (such as arugula and red sorrel), for garnish
Small cilantro sprigs, for garnish
Handful of edible flowers (such as calendula, nasturtiums, and/or pansies), for garnish

Preparation

SALAD

Place the peppers on the cooking grid and close the lid of the EGG. Cook, turning as needed, for several minutes, until charred on all sides. Remove the peppers from the EGG, let cool until they can be handled, then peel away the skin. Halve lengthwise, remove the seeds, and cut into long, narrow strips. Set aside.

Place the hazelnuts in the ovenproof frying pan on the cooking grid, close the lid of the EGG, and cook, stirring and checking occasionally, until toasted. This should take only a few minutes. Chop coarsely and set aside.

CHICKEN LIVERS

Trim away any membranes or dark spots from the livers, then pat dry. Cut the livers into ¾-inch (2-cm) square pieces. Set aside. Place the garlic, red pepper flakes, soaked saffron, and some oil in the frying pan on the cooking grid, close the lid of the EGG, and fry for a few minutes, until fragrant and the garlic is golden. Add the orange blossom water and Cognac, stir to mix, and season with the fleur de sel. Set aside.

Place the Perforated Cooking Grid in the EGG and close the lid to preheat. Sprinkle the livers liberally with the lavender salt, place them on the hot Grid, close the lid of the EGG, and cook for 2 to 3 minutes on each side, until russet colored on the outside and slightly pink on the inside. (Using the Perforated Cooking Grid will prevent the liver pieces from falling into the coals.)

TO FINISH

Mix the chicken livers with the reserved garlic-saffron mixture. Drizzle with the lemon juice. Make a bed of the bell pepper strips on a serving plate and top with the livers. Garnish with the hazelnuts, greens, cilantro, and flowers.

EQUIPMENT

Handful of apple or other fragrant wood chips, soaked in water for at least 30 minutes

GRILL TEMPERATURE

Set the EGG for direct cooking without the grid. Preheat the EGG to 195°F (90°C).

COOKING TIME

4 minutes
(+ 15 minutes to cook the lentils)

SERVES 6

LENTILS with smoked lemon dressing

This lemon dressing is versatile and is equally delicious with fish, chicken, or lamb. It can also be paired with lemon curd for a special dessert.

Ingredients

SMOKED LEMON DRESSING

4 lemons, halved

1 clove garlic

Salt and freshly ground black pepper

1 teaspoon sugar

Scant ½ cup (100 ml) extra-virgin olive oil

LENTILS

4¼ cups (1 L) water

2 cups (500 g) French green lentils

1 bay leaf

3 celery ribs, thinly sliced

4 tomatoes, cut into chunks

Coarsely chopped fresh mint, for seasoning

Coarsely chopped fresh cilantro, for seasoning

Coarsely chopped fresh dill, for seasoning

Coarsely chopped fresh flat-leaf parsley, for seasoning

1 red onion, thinly sliced

7 ounces (200 g) feta cheese, crumbled

Preparation

SMOKED LEMON DRESSING

Scatter the wood chips over the hot coals and place the cooking grid in the EGG. Place the lemons, cut side down, on the grid, close the lid of the EGG, and smoke the lemons for 4 minutes. Squeeze the juice from the lemon halves into a small bowl and add some of the pulp, as well. Using a fine-rasp grater, grate the garlic into the lemon juice and pulp. Add the sugar, season with salt and pepper, and mix well. In a blender, whirl the olive oil a few times on low speed. Add the blended oil to the lemon mixture and mix well.

LENTILS

Bring the water to a boil in a saucepan over high heat on the stove top. Add the lentils and bay leaf, turn down the heat to medium, and cook for about 15 minutes, or until al dente. Drain the lentils, discarding the bay leaf, and transfer to a large bowl. Add the celery, tomatoes, herbs, and onion and stir and toss to mix.

TO FINISH

Drizzle the dressing over the lentil salad and toss to coat evenly. Sprinkle the feta over the top.

COOKING TIME

50 to 60 minutes

(+ overnight to marinate)

GRILL TEMPERATURE

Set the EGG for direct cooking
with the Cast Iron Grid.
Preheat the EGG to 350°F (180°C).

EQUIPMENT

Cast Iron Grid

Instant-read thermometer

BUTTERFLIED CHICKEN
with lots of spices and tahini mayonnaise

This way of preparing chicken is popular with grilling enthusiasts and rivals the popular "chicken under a brick." Here, the backbone of the chicken is removed so the bird will lie flat on the grid. If you like, you can top the chicken with a brick or secure it with skewers to make sure it stays flat and cooks evenly. Accompany with Lentils with Smoked Lemon Dressing (page 52).

Ingredients

Preparation

CHICKEN

2 small shallots, chopped

4 cloves garlic, minced

1-inch (2.5-cm) piece fresh ginger, peeled and grated

Grated zest and juice of 2 oranges

4 tablespoons sumac

4 tablespoons paprika

4 tablespoons red pepper flakes

4 tablespoons ground cumin

Several fresh marjoram or oregano leaves, plus sprigs for garnish

Dash of brandy

Scant ½ cup (100 ml) olive oil

Pinch of salt

Pinch of freshly ground black pepper

2 (3¼-pound / 1.5-kg) whole chickens

1 orange, peeled and sliced

TAHINI MAYONNAISE

1 egg yolk, at room temperature

1½ tablespoons fresh lemon juice

Salt and freshly ground black pepper

1 cup (240 ml) olive oil

2 tablespoons tahini

CHICKEN

In a small bowl, combine the shallots, garlic, ginger, orange zest and juice, sumac, paprika, red pepper flakes, cumin, marjoram leaves, brandy, oil, salt, and pepper and mix well.

You can ask the butcher to remove the backbone from the chickens or you can do it yourself. To do it yourself, turn each chicken breast side down. Using poultry shears or sharp kitchen scissors and starting alongside the tail, cut straight up to the neck end. Then, starting along the other side of the tail, cut straight up again to the neck and lift away the backbone. Turn the chicken breast side up, press down firmly on the breastbone until the chicken lies flat, and tuck in the wings. Using a knife with a thin, flexible blade, loosen the skin from the flesh as much as possible. Rub the herb-spice mixture both under and on top of the skin. Slip the orange slices under the skin. Place the chickens in a covered container and marinate overnight in the refrigerator.

TAHINI MAYONNAISE

Place the egg yolk, lemon juice, and a little salt and pepper in a bowl. Using a handheld mixer, beat until well blended. With the mixer running on high speed, add the oil in a very slow, fine stream and beat until the mixture is thick and smooth. (Once an emulsion has formed, the oil can be added a little more quickly.) Stir in the tahini.

TO FINISH

Place the chickens, breast side down, on the Cast Iron Grid, close the lid of the EGG, and cook for 10 to 15 minutes, until a nice crust has formed. Turn the chickens over, close the lid of the EGG, and cook for another 40 to 45 minutes, until an instant-read thermometer inserted in the thigh away from bone registers 165°F (74°C). Garnish the chickens with marjoram sprigs and serve with the mayonnaise.

DISCO CHARD
with salsa verde

Growers at farmers' markets often give their produce fanciful names. This recipe for disco chard, which pairs different-colored chards with a zesty salsa, plays off that tradition. The sweet, earthy flavor of chard marries well with many foods, such as anchovies and capers, fish, and chicken.

Ingredients

1⅔ pounds (750 g) Swiss chard in a mix of colors

Olive oil, for brushing

SALSA VERDE

1 small bunch flat-leaf parsley, finely chopped

1 small bunch dill, finely chopped

1 small bunch tarragon, finely chopped

1 red bell pepper, seeded and finely chopped

Scant ½ cup (100 ml) olive oil

Grated zest and juice of 1 lemon

1 clove garlic, grated

Salt and freshly ground black pepper

Preparation

CHARD

Cut off the stalk from each chard leaf, keeping the stalks and leaves separate. Bring a saucepan filled with water to a boil over high heat on the stove top. Add the stalks and boil for 5 minutes, until partially cooked. Drain well, pat dry, and brush each stalk on both sides with oil. Lightly brush each leaf on both sides with oil.

Place the stalks and leaves on the Cast Iron Grid and close the lid of the EGG. Cook the stalks for 5 minutes on each side, and cook the leaves for 2 minutes on each side.

SALSA VERDE

Combine the parsley, dill, tarragon, bell pepper, and oil in a bowl and stir to mix. Add the lemon zest and juice and garlic, season with salt and pepper, and mix well.

TO FINISH

Serve the chard with the salsa verde.

EQUIPMENT	GRILL TEMPERATURE	COOKING TIME	SERVES 6
convEGGtor	Set the EGG for indirect cooking	3½ to 4 hours	
Large baking dish	with the Roasting & Drip Pan under	(+ at least 1 hour to marinate)	
	the grid.		
	Preheat the EGG to 200°F (100°C).		

BRAISED BEEF SHORT RIBS in five-spice sauce

Beef short ribs taste best when treated to a long cooking time and a tasty sauce. Here, they are cooked slowly until the meat falls off the bone and then paired with a sauce laced with spices. Tangy sauerkraut and a spicy sambal (Indonesian chili sauce) complement the ribs at the table.

Ingredients

RIBS AND RUB

3 tablespoons ground coffee
3 tablespoons cayenne pepper
3 tablespoons dark brown sugar
Salt and freshly ground black pepper
5½ pounds (2.5 kg) beef short ribs

SAUCE

Dash of olive oil
1 large yellow onion, chopped
2 cloves garlic, chopped
1 red bell pepper, seeded and chopped
3 tablespoons tomato paste
1 (750-ml) bottle red wine
3 star anise pods
3 whole cloves
1 cinnamon stick
2 tablespoons fennel seeds
¼ cup (60 ml) soy sauce
12 small fingerling potatoes, unpeeled
Tangy sauerkraut and sambal, for serving

Preparation

RIBS AND RUB

Combine the coffee, cayenne pepper, and brown sugar in a small bowl, mix well, and season with salt and pepper. Coat the ribs evenly with the rub. Let the ribs marinate for at least 1 hour at room temperature or for longer in the refrigerator.

Place the ribs on the cooking grid, close the lid of the EGG, and cook, turning every so often, for 1 to 1½ hours, until nicely browned on all sides. Remove the ribs from the EGG and cover with aluminum foil to keep warm while you prepare the sauce.

SAUCE

Raise the EGG temperature to 350°F (180°C). Place the oil, onion, garlic, and bell pepper in the baking dish, place the dish on the grid, close the lid of the EGG, and heat for a few minutes, until the vegetables begin to soften. Add the tomato paste, wine, spices, and soy sauce and stir to mix. Place the ribs on top of the vegetables, cover the dish with aluminum foil, and close the lid of the EGG. Let the ribs cook for another 2½ hours, or until very tender and the meat easily pulls from the bones. Add the potatoes to the sauce 45 minutes before the ribs are done.

TO FINISH

Serve the ribs, potatoes, and sauce with the sauerkraut and sambal.

SERVES 6	COOKING TIME	GRILL TEMPERATURE	EQUIPMENT
	5 minutes	Set the EGG for direct cooking with	Half Moon Cast Iron Griddle
	(+ 10 minutes to cook	the Half Moon Cast Iron Griddle.	(smooth side)
	the rhubarb)	Preheat the EGG to 350°F (180°C).	

Different types of mackerel, such as king or Spanish, work well with this recipe. Typically mackerel release their eggs in April and May before putting their weight back on in June. Serve this dish in June or later to take advantage of the larger, fattier fish available. The sour chutney nicely complements the richness of the mackerel.

MACKEREL
with plum-soy sauce and rhubarb chutney

Ingredients

RHUBARB CHUTNEY
1 pound (450 g) rhubarb
Grated zest and juice of 2 oranges
2 star anise pods
4 green cardamom pods
1 small red chile, seeded and finely chopped
1-inch (2.5-cm) piece fresh ginger, peeled and finely grated
2 cloves garlic, finely grated
4 tablespoons sugar
2 teaspoons salt

MACKEREL
2 tablespoons sweet soy sauce (ketjap manis)
3 tablespoons Asian plum sauce
6 (6-ounce/170-g) skin-on mackerel fillets
Sunflower oil, for brushing
Few fresh shiso or mint leaves, finely chopped, for finishing
Maldon or other flake sea salt, for finishing

Preparation

RHUBARB CHUTNEY
Use bright red rhubarb, if available, for a colorful dish. Remove and discard the leaves and any strings from each stalk, then cut the stalks into small chunks (this will give the chutney structure). Mix together the rhubarb, orange zest and juice, star anise, cardamom, and chile in a medium saucepan and place over low heat on the stove top. Strew the ginger, garlic, sugar, and salt over the top and cook slowly, stirring occasionally to prevent sticking, for about 10 minutes, or until tender but still slightly firm. Keep warm for later service.

MACKEREL
In a small bowl, stir together the sweet soy and plum sauce. With a sharp knife, cut incisions into the skin side of each mackerel fillet, making a diamond pattern. Rub the skin of each fillet with the soy–plum sauce mixture and brush lightly with the oil. Place the fillets, skin side down, on the Half Moon Cast Iron Griddle, smooth side up, close the lid of the EGG, and cook for about 5 minutes, or until the flesh just flakes when tested with a knife tip.

TO FINISH
Sprinkle the shiso and sea salt over the fillets. Serve with the warm chutney.

Note: This chutney freezes well and is excellent served with pork (see recipe on page 112).

EQUIPMENT	GRILL TEMPERATURE	COOKING TIME	SERVES 6
convEGGtor	Set the EGG for indirect cooking.	1½ hours	
Cedar wood plank, soaked in water	Preheat the EGG to 200°F (100°C).	(+ overnight to marinate and 1 hour to dry,	
for at least 1 hour		10 minutes to cook the beets, and 10 to	
		15 minutes to cook the potatoes)	

smoked warm
SALMON ON BEETS

with beet and fava bean salad topped with horseradish sauce

This dish needs to marinate and dry properly, so be sure to allow sufficient preparation time. It is definitely worth the wait! The traditional Russian flavors of dill, beets, and horseradish sauce pair well with a cold glass of vodka.

Ingredients

MARINATED SALMON
1 large beet, grated
3 tablespoons olive oil
Grated zest of 4 oranges
6 tablespoons (55 g) light brown sugar
3 tablespoons coarse sea salt
3 tablespoons fennel seeds
3 tablespoons coriander seeds
Freshly ground black pepper
1 (2⅔-pound/1.2-kg) salmon fillet
Few bay leaves

HORSERADISH SAUCE
⅔-inch (17-mm) piece fresh horseradish root, peeled and grated
Grated zest of 1 lemon
1 cup (200 g) crème fraîche
Salt and freshly ground black pepper

BEET SALAD
8 medium beets in a mix of colors (such as red, yellow, and Chioggia)
Olive oil, for rubbing and seasoning
12 small fingerling potatoes, unpeeled
1 pound (450 g) fava beans in the pod, shelled
Juice of 1 lemon
1 Granny Smith apple
Fleur de sel and freshly ground black pepper
Few dill sprigs, for topping

Preparation

MARINATED SALMON
In a small bowl, combine the beet, oil, orange zest, sugar, salt, fennel seeds, and coriander seeds, season with pepper, and mix well. Rub this mixture onto the salmon, coating evenly, and arrange the bay leaves on top of the salmon. Wrap the salmon in aluminum foil and marinate in the refrigerator overnight. The following day, unwrap the fish, discard the marinade, and allow the fish to dry, uncovered, for 1 hour in the refrigerator.

Place the cedar plank on the grid, close the lid of the EGG, and leave for a few minutes to heat the plank. Then, carefully turn the plank over and place the salmon on it. Close the lid of the EGG and cook the salmon for 1½ hours.

HORSERADISH SAUCE
In a small bowl, combine the horseradish, lemon zest, and crème fraîche, season with salt and pepper, and mix well.

BEET SALAD
If using yellow beets, do not cook them, as they will be served raw. If using red and/or Chioggia beets, cook them, unpeeled, in a saucepan of boiling water on the stove top for 10 minutes, then drain and pat dry. Rub the dried beets with oil, wrap in aluminum foil, and lay them directly on the hot coals while the salmon is cooking. Their skins will pop.

Bring a medium saucepan filled with water to a boil on the stove top. Add the potatoes, turn down the heat to a simmer, and cook for 10 to 15 minutes, until just tender.

Bring a small saucepan filled with water to a boil on the stove top. Add the fava beans and boil for 3 minutes. Drain, let cool, then remove their outer skins.

If using yellow beets, use a mandoline, cheese slicer, or sharp knife to slice them thinly. Sprinkle the slices with some of the lemon juice. Thinly slice the apple the same way, then sprinkle with the lemon juice.

Peel the red and/or Chioggia beets, cut into chunks, and place in a medium bowl. Add the potatoes, fava beans, and yellow beets and season with oil, fleur de sel, and pepper. Top with the dill and apple slices.

TO FINISH
Cut the salmon into individual servings and accompany with the beet salad and horseradish sauce.

MAKES 3 CALZONE	COOKING TIME	GRILL TEMPERATURE	EQUIPMENT
	25 to 30 minutes per calzone	Set the EGG for indirect cooking with	convEGGtor
	(+ 1½ hours for the dough to rise)	the Pizza & Baking Stone on the grid.	Pizza & Baking Stone
		Preheat the EGG to 425°F (220°C).	Italian Calzone Press
			Dough Rolling Mat or flat work surface
			Pizza Peel or rimless baking sheet

Calzone are popular in southern Italy, particularly in Puglia and Naples. The fillings vary from region to region, but all the versions are delicious, especially when ricotta is included. In the wintertime, try adding broccoli rabe to the filling. Accompany the calzone with an arugula salad.

CALZONE
WITH SAUSAGE AND RICOTTA

Ingredients

PIZZA DOUGH

3 tablespoons crumbled fresh yeast
(1⅓ ounces / 35 g)
2 tablespoons sugar
2¾ cups (650 ml) water, lukewarm
(90° to 100°F / 32° to 38°C)
¼ cup (60 ml) olive oil
8 cups (1 kg) all-purpose flour
1 tablespoon fine sea salt

FILLING

2 cloves garlic, finely chopped
Few fresh tarragon leaves, coarsely chopped
3⅓ cups (500 g) cherry tomatoes
3 tablespoons fennel seeds
Dash of olive oil
3 dried chiles, crumbled
1 pound (450 g) spicy lamb or beef sausages
1½ cups (350 g) ricotta cheese
1 egg, beaten
½ cup (50 g) grated Parmesan cheese
Juice of 1 lemon
Freshly grated nutmeg, for seasoning
Salt and freshly ground black pepper

1 egg yolk, beaten, for brushing
Cornmeal, for dusting

Preparation

PIZZA DOUGH

In a medium bowl, mix the yeast and sugar into the water, stirring until dissolved. Stir in the oil and set aside for 5 to 10 minutes, until foamy. Sift the flour with the salt into a mound on a clean, flat work surface or into a large bowl. Form a small well in the center of the mound and pour the reserved yeast-sugar mixture into the well. Using a wooden spoon, slowly work the flour mixture into the yeast mixture. When the mixture is too heavy to work with a spoon, switch to your hands and knead until a supple dough forms. Coat a large bowl with flour and transfer the dough to the bowl. Cover the bowl with a damp kitchen towel and let the dough rise in a warm place for about 1½ hours, or until doubled in size. Just before using, turn out the dough onto a lightly floured surface and knead several times to remove any air bubbles.

FILLING

In a medium bowl, combine the garlic, tarragon, cherry tomatoes (keep the tomatoes whole to prevent excess moisture inside the calzone), fennel seeds, oil, and chiles and stir gently to mix.

Cut the sausages into chunks or remove from the casings and crumble coarsely. Place in a frying pan over medium-high heat on the stove top and fry just until browned. Transfer to paper towels to drain briefly. (Do not overcook, as the sausage will continue to cook in the EGG.) In a small bowl, stir together the ricotta, egg,

Parmesan, and lemon juice and season with nutmeg, salt, and pepper. Add the sausage and ricotta mixture to the tomato mixture and mix gently but thoroughly.

TO FINISH

Divide the dough into 3 equal portions and flatten each portion into a disk. Place a disk on the Dough Rolling Mat or a lightly floured work surface and, using a floured rolling pin, roll out into a large, thin piece (about ⅛ inch / 3 mm thick). Use the bottom of the open Italian Calzone Press to cut out a circle from the dough. Transfer the dough circle onto the concave side of the Press. Spread one-third of the filling onto one side of the dough circle. Dampen the edges of the dough circle with water, then close the Press firmly to seal securely. Repeat with the remaining dough and filling. You may have dough left over, but the motto, "Better to have too much than too little," applies here. Brush the outside of each calzone with the egg yolk wash.

Dust the Pizza Peel or sheet pan with cornmeal, lift a calzone onto the Peel, and slide the calzone onto the preheated Pizza & Baking Stone. (If your EGG will accommodate more than a single calzone, add a second one.) Close the lid of the EGG and bake for 25 to 30 minutes, until golden brown. Using the Peel, remove the calzone from the EGG. Serve immediately. Repeat with the remaining calzone.

EQUIPMENT
convEGGtor
Roasting & Drip Pan
Meat thermometer
Grill Gripper

GRILL TEMPERATURE
Set the EGG for indirect cooking with
the Roasting & Drip Pan under the grid.
Preheat the EGG to 350°F (180°C).

COOKING TIME
55 minutes
(+ 15 minutes to rest)

SERVES 6

GRILLED TOP SIRLOIN STEAK
with roasted carrots and spelt salad

This recipe is inspired by a popular Brazilian beef cut, the *picanha*, which is traditionally grilled. Here, a top sirloin steak is used, but if you want to prepare a more authentic version, seek out a rump cap roast. Grill the meat as one piece or as steaks 1 inch (2.5 cm) thick.

Ingredients

TOP SIRLOIN STEAK
1 (2-pound/1-kg) top sirloin steak with fat cap, at room temperature
Coarse sea salt and freshly ground black pepper
Roasted Carrot Salad with Spelt and Carrot Dressing (page 73)

Preparation

TOP SIRLOIN STEAK
Place the meat, fat side up, on a work surface. Using a sharp knife, score the fat with a diamond pattern. Rub both the fat and meat of the steak with salt and let rest for 5 minutes, then remove most of the salt.

Insert the meat thermometer into the meat and place the meat, fat side up, on the cooking grid. Close the lid of the EGG and cook the meat for 50 minutes, or until the thermometer registers 135°F (57°C) for medium-rare.

TO FINISH
Remove the meat from the EGG. Using the Grill Gripper, remove the grid and then carefully remove the Roasting & Drip Pan and convEGGtor. Replace the cooking grid in the EGG, and place the meat, fat side down, on the grid for a few more minutes, until nice and crusty. Tent the meat with aluminum foil and let rest for 10 minutes. Slice the steak against the grain and serve with the carrot salad.

SERVES 6	COOKING TIME	GRILL TEMPERATURE	EQUIPMENT
	5 minutes	Set the EGG for direct cooking.	Deep Dish Pizza/Baking Stone
	(+ 30 to 45 minutes to cook	Preheat the EGG to 395°F (200°C).	or baking dish
	the spelt and the carrot for the		
	dressing)		

This colorful salad roasts purple, yellow, and black carrots until their sugars lightly caramelize, and then combines them with earthy spelt and a thick dressing that marries carrot, fresh oregano, ginger, naturally sweet orange juice, and olive oil.

ROASTED CARROT SALAD
with spelt and carrot dressing

Ingredients

SPELT AND CARROT DRESSING
2⅓ cups (400 g) spelt berries
Salt
1 large orange carrot, peeled and cut into chunks
Small knob fresh ginger, peeled
1 clove garlic
Juice of 1 orange
Few fresh oregano leaves
Salt and freshly ground black pepper
Olive oil, for seasoning

ROASTED CARROTS
1 to 2 bunches small carrots in a mix of colors, unpeeled and with stems intact
Handful of watercress sprigs, for garnish
Lemon wedges, for serving

Preparation

SPELT AND CARROT DRESSING
Bring a medium saucepan filled with lightly salted water to a boil. Add the spelt berries, turn down the heat to a simmer, and cook for 30 to 45 minutes, until tender but still chewy. Drain and set aside. Meanwhile, bring a small saucepan filled with water to a boil, add the carrot and ginger, and cook for about 10 minutes, or until tender. Remove and discard the ginger, then drain the carrot, reserving the cooking water. Transfer the carrot to a blender, add the garlic, orange juice, and a little of the cooking water, and process until a thick dressing forms. Season with the oregano, salt, pepper, and oil.

TO FINISH
Place the colored carrots in the Deep Dish Pizza/Baking Stone or the baking dish, place on the cooking grid, close the lid of the EGG, and roast for about 5 minutes, or until al dente. Cut the roasted carrots into chunks or leave whole if small. Toss the reserved spelt with the dressing, arrange on a platter, and top with the roasted carrots. Garnish with the watercress and accompany with the lemon wedges.

EQUIPMENT
Half Moon Cast Iron Griddle
(smooth side)

GRILL TEMPERATURE
Set the EGG for direct cooking with
the Half Moon Cast Iron Griddle.
Preheat the EGG to 475°F (240°C).

COOKING TIME
6 minutes
(+ 30 minutes to cook the split peas)

SERVES 6

SQUID FROM THE PLANCHA

with chorizo and puréed yellow split peas

Squid cooked quickly on a hot griddle with some olive oil, salt, and pepper is quite tasty, provided you prepare it correctly. The trick is to clean the squid thoroughly and not to overcook it. A variation of this dish is a specialty on the Greek island of Santorini, where the volcanic soil produces nutty-flavored yellow split peas.

Ingredients

SPLIT PEA PURÉE
1¾ cups (350 g) yellow split peas, rinsed
1 yellow onion, quartered
1 clove garlic
2 fresh bay leaves
Scant ½ cup (100 ml) olive oil
Juice of 2 lemons
Salt and freshly ground black pepper

SQUID AND CHORIZO
6 (7-ounce/200-g) squid (about 2⅔ pounds/
1.2 kg total)
Fine sea salt and freshly ground black pepper
Dash of olive oil
1 (5½-ounce/155-g) piece chorizo, sliced and
then slices quartered
4 green onions, thinly sliced
2 lemons, halved

Preparation

SPLIT PEA PURÉE
Place the peas, onion, garlic, and bay leaves in a medium saucepan and add water to cover by 1 inch (2.5 cm). Place on the stove top over medium-high heat, bring to a boil, turn down the heat to low, and cook for about 30 minutes, or until the peas are tender. Drain the peas, reserving the cooking liquid. Discard only the bay leaves.

In a blender, combine the peas, oil, lemon juice, and a little of the cooking liquid and process until smooth. Season with salt and pepper and set aside.

SQUID AND CHORIZO
To clean each squid, hold the head in one hand and the body in the other and gently pull the head away from the body; the entrails should pull away, too. Sever the tentacles from the head, cutting just below the eyes, and discard the head and entrails. Remove and discard the beak from the center of the tentacles and set the tentacles aside. Pull the long, thin sliver of cartilage from the body tube and discard, then rinse the inside of the tube well. Holding the body tube under running water, rub or scrape off the mottled purplish skin, leaving the meat white. When all of the squid are cleaned, cut a small V shape in the top of each body. Season the bodies and tentacles with sea salt, pepper, and oil.

Place the squid bodies on the Half Moon Cast Iron Griddle, smooth side up, close the lid of the EGG, and cook for 2 to 3 minutes per side. Place the tentacles on the Griddle when the bodies are almost ready, as they do not require much time. Cook the chorizo alongside the squid on the Griddle.

TO FINISH
Spoon the split pea purée onto a plate and scatter the green onions over the purée. Squeeze the lemon halves over the squid. Serve the squid and chorizo atop the split pea purée.

SERVES 6	COOKING TIME	GRILL TEMPERATURE	EQUIPMENT
	2½ hours	Set the EGG for indirect cooking.	convEGGtor
	(+ overnight to marinate the ribs	Preheat the EGG to 320°F (160°C).	V-Rack
	and 30 minutes to 1 hour for the		Rectangular Roasting & Drip Pan or
	dough to rest)		large baking dish
			Grill Gripper

The inspiration for the Big Green Egg originated with the ancient Chinese clay oven and the Japanese kamado. But the EGG also works similarly to the Indian tandoor oven, which is used primarily for preparing meats and flatbreads. Here, the EGG is used for cooking chapatis, unleavened pancake-like Indian breads. They bake from the heat of the inside walls, so before starting, clean the walls thoroughly. Alternatively, bake the chapatis on the Pizza & Baking Stone.

INDIAN
LAMB SPARERIBS
with chapatis and apple yogurt

Ingredients

LAMB SPARERIBS
8 cloves garlic
2-inch (5-cm) piece fresh ginger, peeled
4 tablespoons cayenne pepper
4 tablespoons ground green cardamom
2 whole nutmeg seeds, grated
4 tablespoons cumin seeds
4 tablespoons garam masala (Indian spice blend)
Salt and freshly ground black pepper
½ cup (100 g) plain Greek yogurt
Juice of 1 lemon
5½ to 6½ pounds (2.5 to 3 kg) lamb spareribs

APPLE YOGURT
1 Granny Smith apple, grated
⅔-inch (17-mm) piece fresh ginger, peeled and grated
1¼ cups (250 g) plain Greek yogurt
1 tablespoon sunflower oil
1 tablespoon mustard seeds
1 teaspoon ground turmeric or saffron
Salt and freshly ground black pepper
Chopped fresh cilantro, for seasoning

CHAPATIS
1⅔ cups (200 g) all-purpose flour
1⅔ cups (200 g) whole wheat flour
1 teaspoon salt
1 tablespoon olive oil
1⅓ cups (320 ml) warm water

Preparation

LAMB SPARERIBS
Using a fine-rasp grater held over a small bowl, grate the garlic and ginger into a pulp. Add the cayenne pepper, cardamom, nutmeg, cumin, garam masala, big pinch of salt, a few grinds of pepper, the yogurt, and the lemon juice and mix well. Coat the ribs evenly with the mixture, cover, and marinate overnight in the refrigerator.

APPLE YOGURT
In a small bowl, combine the apple, ginger, and yogurt and mix well. Heat the sunflower oil in a small frying pan over low heat on the stove top. Add the mustard seeds and heat until the seeds dance in the oil. Add the turmeric and heat a little longer until fragrant, then remove from the heat and add to the yogurt mixture. Season with salt and pepper, stir in the cilantro to taste, and set aside.

BAKING THE RIBS
Place the ribs in the V-Rack and set the V-Rack in the Roasting & Drip Pan or baking dish to catch the drippings (the drippings make a delicious sauce that can be served with the ribs). Place the Roasting & Drip Pan on the grid, close the lid of the EGG, and cook the ribs for 2 to 2½ hours, until tender.

Remove the V-Rack and Roasting & Drip Pan with the ribs from the EGG, use the Grill Gripper to remove the grid, and then carefully remove the convEGGtor. Place the cooking grid in the EGG and increase the temperature to 525°F (275°C). Place the ribs on the grid, close the lid of the EGG, and grill the lamb for 5 more minutes on each side for a nice crust.

CHAPATIS
In a large bowl, stir together both flours and the salt. Add the oil and then add the water, a small amount at a time, gradually working it into the dry ingredients until fully incorporated. Knead in the bowl until a smooth, elastic dough forms. Shape the dough into a ball, place in a bowl, cover, and let rest at room temperature for 30 minutes to 1 hour.

Remove the grid and increase the EGG temperature to 570°F (300°C). Divide the dough into 10 equal portions. On a floured work surface, roll out each portion into a thin round about 6 inches (15 cm) in diameter. Using tongs, hold each round against the inner rim of the EGG to bake for 1 to 2 minutes per side. Then, hold each chapati directly over the flames briefly until it starts to curl a bit.

TO FINISH
Serve the ribs with the yogurt and hot chapatis.

EQUIPMENT

Handful of cherry or other fragrant wood chips, soaked in water for at least 30 minutes

Half Moon Cast Iron Griddle (smooth side)

GRILL TEMPERATURE

Set the EGG for direct cooking without the grid. Preheat the EGG to 250°F (120°C).

COOKING TIME

35 minutes

SERVES 6

GRILLED CABBAGE AND SMOKED PURÉE
with blue cheese, butter sauce, and sage chips

Here is a sophisticated dish that marries the autumn flavors of red cabbage, sage, and apples. If you cannot locate the Cabrales cheese, substitute Roquefort or Gorgonzola.

Ingredients

SMOKED PURÉE
2¼ pounds (1 kg) potatoes, peeled and quartered
⅔ cup (150 ml) whole milk
4 tablespoons unsalted butter, at room temperature
1 cup (100 g) grated pecorino or Parmesan cheese
1 teaspoon freshly grated nutmeg
Salt and freshly ground black pepper

BUTTER SAUCE
¾ cup (200 g) unsalted butter

GRILLED CABBAGE
1 red cabbage
Olive oil, for brushing
Salt and freshly ground black pepper
14 ounces (400 g) Cabrales, Roquefort, or Gorgonzola cheese, crumbled

APPLES AND SAGE CHIPS
2 tart apples, sliced
Handful of fresh sage leaves
Salt

Preparation

SMOKED PURÉE
Bring a large saucepan filled with water to a boil on the stove top. Add the potatoes, boil for 5 minutes, and drain. Scatter the wood chips over the hot coals and place the cooking grid in the EGG. Place the potatoes on the grid, close the lid of the EGG, and smoke the potatoes for 15 to 20 minutes, until tender. Transfer the potatoes to a medium bowl, add the milk, butter, and cheese, and mash until a smooth purée forms. Season with the nutmeg, salt, and pepper and keep warm.

BUTTER SAUCE
Melt the butter in a small saucepan on the stove top over medium-low heat. When it starts to foam, stir it occasionally to prevent the milk solids from burning. Continue to heat until the butter has turned a pale nut brown and smells lightly nutty and toasty. Pour off the clear butter into a bowl, leaving the sediment behind. Set aside.

GRILLED CABBAGE
Place the Half Moon Cast Iron Griddle, smooth side up, in the EGG, increase the temperature to 390°F (200°C), and preheat the Griddle. Cut the cabbage in half through the stem end, then cut crosswise into slices ¼ inch (6 mm) thick. Brush the cabbage with oil and sprinkle with salt and pepper. Place the cabbage slices on the Griddle, close the lid of the EGG, and cook for 3 minutes. Turn over the cabbage slices, scatter the cheese on top, close the lid of the EGG, and cook for 3 minutes longer, or until the cheese is melted.

APPLES AND SAGE CHIPS
Brush the apple slices with some of the butter sauce. Set aside the remaining butter sauce. Place the apple slices on the Griddle, close the lid of the EGG, and cook for a few minutes, until soft.

Ladle out about one-fourth of the remaining butter sauce and set aside. Reheat the remaining butter sauce over medium-low heat on the stove top, add the sage leaves, and cook for a few minutes, or until crisp. Using a slotted spoon, transfer the sage leaves to a paper towel to drain. Season with salt.

TO FINISH
Spoon the potato purée onto a plate and top with the cabbage and apples. Drizzle the reserved butter sauce over the top. Serve the sage chips on the side.

SERVES 6	COOKING TIME	GRILL TEMPERATURE	EQUIPMENT
	25 minutes	Set the EGG for indirect cooking without the convEGGtor. Preheat the EGG to 350°F (180°C).	Handful of pecan or other fragrant wood chips, soaked in water for at least 30 minutes convEGGtor 2 Roasting & Drip Pans or large baking dishes Grill Gripper

This dish takes advantage of both the abundant meat found in king crab legs and the flavorful, rich, and buttery contents of the body of a crab. The recipe calls for live crabs, but if only frozen crabs are available in your area, they will do. Serve this dish with a green salad topped with avocado, grapefruit, and crispy fried pancetta.

SMOKED CRAB
with orange-tarragon aioli

Ingredients

ORANGE-TARRAGON AIOLI
1 organic orange
2 egg yolks
3½ tablespoons (50 ml) tarragon vinegar
Salt and freshly ground black pepper
1 large clove garlic, grated
2 cups (480 ml) sunflower oil
Coarsely chopped fresh tarragon leaves, for seasoning

CRAB
3 live crabs
2¼ pounds (1 kg) precooked king crab legs
6½ cups (1.5 L) boiling water
2 cups (480 ml) distilled white vinegar
2 cups (480 ml) beer or apple cider

Preparation

ORANGE-TARRAGON AIOLI

Combine the orange with water to cover in a small saucepan over high heat on the stove top. Bring to a boil and boil until the skin tests soft when pierced with a knife. Drain, cut into quarters, discard any seeds, and transfer to a blender. Whirl on low speed until a smooth pulp forms. Set the pulp aside. To make the aioli, rinse the blender beaker, then combine the egg yolks, vinegar, a little salt and pepper, and the garlic in the blender and process on low speed until well blended. With the blender running continuously, add the oil in a very fine, slow stream and process until the mixture is thick and smooth. (Once an emulsion has formed, the oil can be added a little more quickly.) Transfer the aioli to a medium bowl and stir in the reserved orange pulp and the tarragon to taste. If you have leftover aioli, it will keep in the refrigerator for several days.

CRAB

Make sure you have a big pot filled with plenty of boiling water ready in which to immerse the live crabs before you place them on the grill for smoking. Scatter the wood chips over the hot coals, then place the convEGGtor, with the legs facing up, in the EGG. Divide the boiling water, vinegar, and beer evenly between the 2 Roasting & Drip Pans or baking dishes. Place the Roasting & Drip Pans on the convEGGtor, top with the cooking grid, and close the lid of the EGG. Let the grill get hot; there should be plenty of steam and smoke. Immerse the crabs in the pot of boiling water for 5 minutes. Remove the crabs from the boiling water, place them on the grid, close the lid of the EGG, and steam for 15 to 20 minutes, until cooked. Because the crab legs are precooked, they need only about 10 minutes in the EGG to warm. Remove the crabs and crab legs from the grid. Using the Grill Gripper, remove the grid, then carefully remove the Roasting & Drip Pans from the EGG. Return the grid to the EGG.

Hit the crabs with a hammer so they can absorb the smoke better and return them and the legs to the grid. Close the lid of the EGG and let smoke for 5 minutes.

TO FINISH

Using kitchen scissors, cut each crab leg open at the top of the leg. Serve the crabs and crab legs with the aioli. Don't forget to spoon out the delicious butter inside the whole crabs.

EQUIPMENT

convEGGtor

Pizza & Baking Stone

Dough Rolling Mat or flat work surface

Pizza Peel or rimless baking sheet

GRILL TEMPERATURE

Set the EGG for indirect cooking with the
Pizza & Baking Stone on the grid.
Preheat the EGG from 525° to 570°F
(275° to 300°C).

COOKING TIME

5 to 6 minutes per batch
(+ 1½ hours for the dough to rise and
10 to 15 minutes to cook the topping)

MAKES 12 SMALL PIZZAS

PIZZETTE
with red onion, figs, and
GORGONZOLA

Pizzetta is the Italian diminutive of pizza,
which translates to small, cute pie.
This recipe shows you how to create little
pizzas with delicious toppings.

Ingredients

PIZZA DOUGH

3 tablespoons crumbled fresh yeast
(1⅓ ounces/35 g)

2 tablespoons sugar

2¾ cups (650 ml) water, lukewarm
(90° to 100°F/32° to 38°C)

¼ cup (60 ml) olive oil

8 cups (1 kg) all-purpose flour

1 tablespoon fine sea salt

Cornmeal, for dusting

TOPPING

3 red onions, sliced into rings and rings halved

Dash of olive oil

Several fresh thyme leaves

2½ tablespoons unsalted butter

Salt

Dash of balsamic vinegar

12 fresh figs, sliced crosswise

1 pound (450 g) Gorgonzola cheese, crumbled

1 bunch basil, for garnish

Freshly ground black pepper

Preparation

PIZZA DOUGH

In a medium bowl, mix the yeast and sugar into the water, stirring until dissolved. Stir in the oil and set aside for 5 to 10 minutes, until foamy. Sift the flour with the salt into a mound on a clean, flat work surface or into a large bowl. Form a small well in the center of the mound and pour the reserved yeast-sugar mixture into the well. Using a wooden spoon, slowly work the flour mixture into the yeast mixture. When the mixture is too heavy to work with a spoon, switch to your hands and knead until a supple dough forms. Coat a large bowl with flour and transfer the dough to the bowl. Cover the bowl with a damp kitchen towel and let the dough rise in a warm place for about 1½ hours, or until doubled in size. Just before using, turn out the dough onto a lightly floured surface and knead several times to remove any air bubbles.

TOPPING

Fry the onions in the oil in a frying pan over medium heat on the stove top for a few minutes. Add the thyme and butter, season with salt, and cook, stirring often, for 5 to 8 minutes, until the onions are soft. Add the balsamic vinegar and remove from the heat.

BAKING THE DOUGH

Divide the dough into 12 equal portions and flatten each portion into a disk. Place a disk on the Dough Rolling Mat or a lightly floured work surface and, using a floured rolling pin, roll out into a thin circle. Dust the Pizza Peel or sheet pan with cornmeal and transfer the dough circle to the Peel. Repeat to make a second dough circle and add to the Peel. Top each circle with one-twelfth each of the onions, fig slices, and Gorgonzola. (Or, ready as many pizzette on the Peel as will fit in your EGG at one time.) Gently shake the Peel to make sure the dough is not sticking to it.

Slide the pizzette onto the preheated Stone. Close the lid of the EGG and bake for 5 to 7 minutes, until the edges are crisp and brown.

TO FINISH

Using the Peel, remove the pizzette from the EGG and top with a little basil and a grind of pepper. Serve immediately. Repeat with the remaining dough and toppings.

COOKING TIME

45 minutes

(+ 25 minutes to simmer the milk

and begin the polenta)

GRILL TEMPERATURE

Set the EGG for direct cooking.

Preheat the EGG to 350°F (180°C).

EQUIPMENT

Large baking dish

Dutch Oven or ovenproof frying pan

Grill Gripper

Cast Iron Grid

This recipe is not the poor man's version of polenta. The milk used for cooking it is infused with rosemary and garlic, and fresh corn, butter, and Parmesan are stirred into the polenta. Serve the polenta with a hefty spoonful of Vacherin Mont d'Or, a creamy autumnal cheese available at the end of September through spring.

BAKED POLENTA WITH MUSHROOMS
and melted Vacherin Mont d'Or

Ingredients

POLENTA

3 cloves garlic, mashed

6⅓ cups (1.5 L) low-fat milk

Few rosemary sprigs

1¾ cups (350 g) quick-cooking polenta

1 teaspoon freshly grated nutmeg

Salt and freshly ground pepper

3 tablespoons unsalted butter

¾ cup (75 g) grated Parmesan cheese

Kernels from 2 ears corn

1 Vacherin Mont d'Or or similar French or Swiss cow's milk cheese

MUSHROOMS

1 shallot, diced

1 tablespoon unsalted butter

14 ounces (400 g) chanterelle mushrooms, cleaned

Few thyme or sage sprigs

Dash of sherry

Salt and freshly ground black pepper

Preparation

POLENTA

Combine the garlic, milk, and rosemary in a saucepan over medium-high heat on the stove top and bring just to a boil. Turn down the heat to medium-low and simmer gently for 20 minutes. Pour the milk through a fine-mesh sieve, discarding the garlic and rosemary.

Return the milk to the saucepan and bring to a boil on the stove top. Slowly add the polenta while stirring constantly. Season with the nutmeg, salt, and pepper and continue to stir until the polenta starts to bind and begins to bubble. Add the butter and Parmesan, allow the butter to melt, and then stir in the corn kernels. Empty the polenta into the baking dish .

Place the dish on the cooking grid, close the lid of the EGG, and cook for 20 minutes. Remove the dish from the EGG, let cool, and invert the polenta onto a cutting board. Cut the polenta into individual portions.

MUSHROOMS

Place the Dutch Oven or frying pan on the grid and add the shallot and butter. Close the lid of the EGG and cook for 2 to 3 minutes, until soft. Add the mushrooms, thyme, and sherry, season with salt and pepper, and close the lid. Cook for 10 to 15 minutes, until the mushrooms are tender. Keep warm.

TO FINISH

Use the Grill Gripper to remove the cooking grid, then place the Cast Iron Grid in the EGG and close the lid to preheat.

Place the polenta portions on the hot Grid and close the lid of the EGG. Cook, turning once, to create grill marks on both sides of the polenta, then cook for a few minutes more to heat through.

Divide the cheese into 6 portions and place a portion on top of each serving of warm polenta to melt slightly. Accompany with the mushrooms.

EQUIPMENT

Dutch Oven or ovenproof frying pan

GRILL TEMPERATURE

Set the EGG for direct cooking.
Preheat the EGG to 300°F (150°C).

COOKING TIME

1¼ hours
(+ several hours to steep the vanilla oil)

SERVES 6

BAKED PURPLE POTATOES
with mushrooms and vanilla oil

This side dish is simple and delicious. The combination of mushrooms and vanilla seems unlikely, but they make a perfect marriage. You can also turn this dish into a salad by adding thinly sliced fennel.

Ingredients

VANILLA OIL

2 vanilla beans

2 cloves garlic, lightly mashed

⅔ cup (150 ml) mild olive oil

BAKED POTATOES

1½ pounds (680 g) purple potatoes, unpeeled

Salt

Olive oil, for rubbing

MUSHROOMS

1 shallot, diced

1 tablespoon unsalted butter

1 pound (450 g) mushrooms (such as chanterelle, hedgehog, or black trumpet), cleaned and sliced

Few thyme sprigs

Dash of sherry

Salt and freshly ground black pepper

Preparation

VANILLA OIL

Slit the vanilla beans in half lengthwise and scrape out the seeds. Discard the pods. Combine the vanilla seeds, garlic, and oil in a small covered container and let stand for several hours.

BAKED POTATOES

Sprinkle the potatoes with salt and rub them with oil. Wrap the potatoes in a double layer of aluminum foil. Place the potato packet on the cooking grid, close the lid of the EGG, and bake for 1 hour, or until tender.

MUSHROOMS

Increase the grill temperature to 390°F (200°C). Place the Dutch Oven or frying pan on the grid and add the shallot and butter. Close the lid of the EGG and cook for 2 to 3 minutes, until soft. Add the mushrooms, thyme, and sherry, season with salt and pepper, and close the lid of the EGG. Cook for about 10 minutes, or until the mushrooms are tender.

TO FINISH

Break the potatoes open and serve them with the mushrooms. Pour the reserved vanilla oil over the potatoes and sprinkle with salt.

SERVES 6

COOKING TIME
30 minutes
(+ 10 minutes to rest)

GRILL TEMPERATURE
Set the EGG for direct cooking.
Preheat the EGG to 390°F (200°C).

EQUIPMENT
convEGGtor
Instant-read thermometer
Half Moon Cast Iron Griddle (smooth side)

Prime rib is a favorite of many who enjoy grilling. Use only Angus or other high-quality beef and have it at room temperature. All you need is a little sea salt and freshly ground black pepper and the meat is ready for the grill. The side of porcini mushrooms is a delicious bonus. Or, serve the meat with Baked Purple Potatoes with Mushrooms and Vanilla Oil (page 92).

PRIME RIB
with porcini mushrooms and morel butter

Ingredients

MOREL BUTTER
1 heaping tablespoon dried morels
1 tablespoon peat-flavored Scotch whisky
Dash of water
½ bunch flat-leaf parsley, finely chopped
1 cup (250 g) unsalted butter, at room temperature
Salt and freshly ground black pepper

PRIME RIB
1 (6½-pound/2.7 kg) prime rib (6 bone)
Olive oil, for rubbing
Sea salt and freshly ground black pepper

PORCINI MUSHROOMS
7 ounces (200 g) porcini mushrooms, cleaned
Olive oil, for brushing
Salt and freshly ground black pepper
Few rosemary sprigs

Preparation

MOREL BUTTER
In a bowl, combine the morels, whisky, and water and leave to soak until the mushrooms are rehydrated. Drain the mushrooms, pat dry, and chop finely. Combine the morels, parsley, and butter in a bowl and work them together until the morels and parsley are evenly distributed. Season with salt and pepper, then transfer the butter to a sheet of aluminum foil, shape into a log, and wrap tightly in the foil. Refrigerate until serving.

PRIME RIB
Cut the rib roast between the bones into individual steaks and bring to room temperature. Rub with the oil and sprinkle with sea salt and pepper. Place the steaks on the cooking grid, close the lid of the EGG, and cook for 5 minutes on each side to create nice grill marks. Remove the steaks. Using the Grill Gripper, remove the grid.

Place the convEGGtor, with the legs facing up, in the EGG and top with the cooking grid. Place the steaks on the grid, close the lid of the EGG, and cook for about 15 minutes, or until the instant-read thermometer registers 135°F (57°C) for medium-rare. Remove the steaks from the EGG, tent with aluminum foil, and let rest for 10 minutes before serving.

PORCINI MUSHROOMS
Place the Half Moon Cast Iron Griddle, smooth side up, on top of the grid and close the lid to preheat. Brush the mushrooms with a little oil and sprinkle with salt and pepper. Place the mushrooms and rosemary sprigs on the Griddle, close the lid of the EGG, and cook the mushrooms for a few minutes on both sides, until tender.

TO FINISH
Slice the morel butter and top each steak with a slice. Accompany with the mushrooms.

COOKING TIME

30 minutes

(+ 1 hour for the dough to rest and
1 hour to marinate the pumpkin)

GRILL TEMPERATURE

Set the EGG for indirect cooking with the Deep Dish Pizza/Baking Stone or springform pan on the grid. Preheat the EGG to 350°F (180°C).

EQUIPMENT

convEGGtor

Deep Dish Pizza/Baking Stone or 8½-inch (21.5-cm) springform pan

This tart is a great dessert for a fall barbecue meal. It is served with a touch of creamy Gorgonzola or crème fraîche—an ideal finish for anyone who does not like overly sweet desserts.

PUMPKIN TARTE TATIN
with Gorgonzola dolcelatte or crème fraîche

Ingredients

PIE SHELL*

2 cups (250 g) all-purpose flour

⅓ cup (60 g) sugar

1 teaspoon salt

½ cup plus 1 tablespoon (125 g) unsalted butter, cold, cut into cubes

1 egg yolk

PUMPKIN

1 small pumpkin

Juice of ½ lemon

1-inch (2.5-cm) piece fresh ginger, peeled and grated

1 teaspoon freshly grated nutmeg

1 teaspoon ground green cardamom

CARAMEL

1½ cups (300 g) sugar

Juice of ½ lemon

⅔ cup (150 g) unsalted butter

Gorgonzola dolcelatte cheese or crème fraîche, for serving

* If using the Deep Dish Pizza/Baking Stone, multiply the ingredients by 1½.

Preparation

PIE SHELL

Stir together the flour, sugar, and salt in a medium bowl. Scatter the butter over the flour mixture and, using a pastry blender or two knives, cut the butter into the flour mixture until the mixture resembles coarse meal. Form the mixture into a small mound on a clean work surface, make a well in the center, and add the egg yolk to the well. Gradually work the egg yolk into the flour mixture until a smooth dough comes together. If the dough remains crumbly, add cold water, a little at a time. Be careful not to overwork the dough or the pastry will be tough. Form into a ball, place in a bowl, cover, and let rest in a cool place for 1 hour.

PUMPKIN

Halve the pumpkin, scoop out and discard the seeds and fibers, and then peel the halves. Cut the halves into thin half-moons. Place the pumpkin slices in a bowl, sprinkle with the lemon juice, ginger, nutmeg, and cardamom, and toss gently to coat evenly. Let marinate for 1 hour.

CARAMEL

With the lid of the EGG open, place the sugar in the hot Deep Dish Pizza/Baking Stone or the springform pan in the EGG and stir constantly until the sugar darkens and burns just slightly. Slowly add the lemon juice; the sugar will start to caramelize and bubble. Add the butter and allow it to melt.

BAKING

Carefully remove the Deep Dish Stone from the EGG. Arrange the pumpkin slices in a circle on the caramel. On a lightly floured work surface, roll out the dough into a thin circle slightly larger in diameter than the Deep Dish Stone. Carefully transfer the dough circle to the Deep Dish Stone, drape it over the pumpkin, and tuck it into the sides, pressing firmly. Place the Deep Dish Stone on the grid, close the lid of the EGG, and bake for about 30 minutes, or until golden brown.

TO FINISH

Invert the tarte onto a serving plate. Serve warm with the cheese.

EQUIPMENT

Cast Iron Grid

GRILL TEMPERATURE

Set the EGG for direct cooking with
the Cast Iron Grid.
Preheat the EGG to 390°F (200°C).

COOKING TIME

4 to 6 minutes

(+ 1½ hours to come to room
temperature and to marinate)

SERVES 6

Chimichurri is popular in a broad swath of South America. From Uruguay to the most southern tip of Argentina, everyone has his or her own version of this sauce, which also serves as a marinade. Make the *chimichurri* a few hours ahead of time so the flavors meld and gain more intensity. The sauce will keep in the refrigerator for at least a week.

LAMB CUTLETS
with mint chimichurri

Ingredients

CHIMICHURRI

3½ tablespoons water

1 tablespoon coarse sea salt

2 cloves garlic

1 red bell pepper, seeded and finely chopped

1 large red onion, finely chopped

1 bunch mint, finely chopped

3½ tablespoons red wine vinegar

Scant ½ cup (100 ml) olive oil

2 tablespoons capers

LAMB CUTLETS

12 (4-ounce/115-g) lamb cutlets

½ bunch oregano, chopped

Juice of 2 lemons

Salt and freshly ground black pepper

Olive oil, for rubbing

Preparation

CHIMICHURRI

Combine the water and salt in a small saucepan over low heat on the stove top to dissolve the salt. Let cool. With a mortar and pestle, mash the garlic to a pulp. In a small bowl, combine the garlic, bell pepper, onion, mint, and reserved salted water and stir to mix. Stir in the vinegar, oil, and capers, mixing well. Place in a cool spot to let the flavors meld.

LAMB CUTLETS

Let the cutlets come to room temperature for 1 hour. In a small bowl, combine the oregano, lemon juice, a little salt, and lots of pepper and mix well. Rub the cutlets with the oregano mixture and let rest for 30 minutes.

TO FINISH

Pat the cutlets dry and rub them with oil. Place the cutlets on the Cast Iron Grid, close the lid of the EGG, and cook for 2 to 3 minutes on each side.

Serve the cutlets immediately with the chimichurri sauce.

SERVES 6

COOKING TIME
5 to 6 minutes per tarte flambée
(+ 30 minutes for the dough to rest
and 45 minutes to cook the beets)

GRILL TEMPERATURE
Set the EGG for indirect cooking
with the Pizza & Baking Stone on the grid.
Preheat the EGG to 475°F (250°C).

EQUIPMENT
convEGGtor
Pizza & Baking Stone
Dough Rolling Mat or flat work surface
Pizza Peel or rimless baking sheet

The *tarte flambée*, as the French call it, is tearing across the northern European restaurant and catering landscape. A staple of the Alsace region, it is comparable to a yeast-free pizza and is traditionally topped with crème fraîche, *fromage blanc*, onions, and bacon. The inspiration for this variation on the original comes from Jacques Jour restaurant in Amsterdam, where the kitchen staff is very creative with its toppings. In Europe, you can find ready-made bases in the freezer section of markets. If you are able to find them where you live, you can skip the dough recipe here.

TARTE FLAMBÉE
with beets, eggs, and cheese

Ingredients

TARTE DOUGH
8 cups (1 kg) all-purpose flour
1 teaspoon salt
6 tablespoons (90 ml) olive oil
2½ cups (600 ml) water, lukewarm
(90° to 100°F/32° to 38°C)

TARTE FLAMBÉE
4 beets
1 tablespoon coarse sea salt
2 bay leaves
Dash of distilled white vinegar
1 pound (450 g) soft cow's milk cheese (such as
Brie or Époisses de Bourgogne)
2 cups (480 g) crème fraîche
6 eggs
Freshly grated nutmeg, for sprinkling
Handful of fresh herbs (such as dill, chervil,
and/or chives), for garnish
Grated fresh horseradish root, for garnish

Preparation

TARTE DOUGH
Stir together the flour and salt in a large bowl. Form a well in the center of the flour and pour the oil and water into the well. Using a wooden spoon, slowly work the flour into the liquid ingredients. When the mixture is too heavy to work with a spoon, switch to your hands and knead until you have a smooth, springy dough that does not stick to your hands. Cover the bowl with a kitchen towel and let the dough rest for at least 30 minutes.

TARTE FLAMBÉE
Combine the beets, salt, bay leaves, vinegar, and water to cover in a medium saucepan and bring to a boil over high heat on the stove top. Turn down the heat to medium and boil gently for about 45 minutes, or until tender. Drain the beets, let cool, and peel. Slice the beets and halve the slices or cut the beets into thin wedges. Set aside. Slice the cheese and reserve. Or, if the cheese is very soft, ready it to spread on the dough with a spoon.

Divide the dough into 6 equal portions and flatten each portion into a disk. Place a disk on the Dough Rolling Mat or a lightly floured work surface and, using a floured rolling pin, roll out into a very thin circle. Transfer the circle to the Pizza Peel or sheet pan. Spread the circle with a thin layer of crème fraîche and top with one-sixth each of the beets and cheese. Break an egg onto the middle of the circle and sprinkle the toppings with nutmeg. Gently shake the Peel to make sure the dough is not sticking to it. (Or, ready as many tarte bases on the Peel as will fit in your EGG at one time.)

Slide the tarte flambée onto the preheated Pizza & Baking Stone. Close the lid of the EGG and bake for 5 to 6 minutes, until golden brown.

TO FINISH
Using the Peel, remove the tarte flambée from the EGG and garnish with the herbs and horseradish. Serve immediately. Repeat with the remaining dough and toppings.

EQUIPMENT

Dutch oven

8 flexible skewers or 16 metal skewers

Half Moon Cast Iron Griddle (smooth side) or baking dish

GRILL TEMPERATURE

Set the EGG for direct cooking.
Preheat the EGG to 390°F (200°C).

COOKING TIME

20 minutes
(+ 1 to 1½ hours for stewing the octopus and 20 minutes to cook the potatoes)

SERVES 6

OCTOPUS ON SKEWERS
WITH BLACK BEAN SAUCE AND POTATO SALAD

This recipe begins by stewing the octopus in an oven to soften its texture. You do not need to use water for this step because the octopus releases moisture as it cooks. The juices from the stew are incredibly delicious and make a great addition to soups and sauces.

Ingredients

OCTOPUS

2 (3⅓-pound/1.5 kg) fresh octopuses

Dash of olive oil

4 cloves garlic

2 bay leaves

4 tablespoons Chinese black bean sauce

POTATO SALAD

1½ pints (450 g) cherry tomatoes

1½ pounds (600 g) small waxy potatoes

1 bunch flat-leaf parsley, finely chopped

3 tablespoons capers

Olive oil, for drizzling

Salt

1 teaspoon chopped pimientos

Juice of 2 lemons

Preparation

To clean each octopus, cut the head from the tentacles just below the eyes. (The head is not used in this recipe, so you can discard it or you can cut away the eyes, remove and discard the innards trapped inside, and peel away the exterior skin. It can then be cooked until tender and reserved for another use.) Locate the hard beak where the tentacles meet and firmly push or cut it out. Rinse the tentacles under running water.

Heat the oil in a Dutch Oven over high heat on the stove top and add the tentacles. When the tentacles start to release their moisture in 7 to 8 minutes (or longer if necessary), turn down the heat to low, add the garlic and bay leaves, cover, and cook for 1 to 1½ hours, until tender.

Or you can preheat the oven to 500°F (260°C). Heat the oil in a Dutch Oven over high heat on the stove top, add the tentacles, and transfer the pot or dish to the hot oven. When the tentacles start to release their moisture in 7 to 8 minutes, lower the oven temperature to 350°F (180°C), add the garlic and bay leaves, cover, and cook for 1 to 1½ hours, until tender.

Let the tentacles cool, then thread them onto the skewers and baste with the black bean sauce. Just before serving, place the tentacles on the cooking grid, close the lid of the EGG, and cook for a few minutes on each side, until they develop a crispy crust.

POTATO SALAD

Place the Half Moon Cast Iron Griddle, smooth side up, or baking dish on the grid and close the lid of the EGG to preheat. Add the tomatoes to the hot Griddle, close the lid, and cook for a few minutes, until the skins start to wrinkle and the tomatoes begin to collapse. Set the tomatoes aside. Bring a large saucepan filled with water to a boil on the stove top, add the potatoes, and cook for about 20 minutes, or until tender when pierced with a fork. Drain the potatoes, transfer to a bowl, and mash coarsely. Add the parsley and capers and then add the tomatoes, mashing them a bit so their juices are released into the potatoes. Drizzle some oil over the potatoes and tomatoes to make a dressing and season with salt. Add the pimientos and stir gently.

TO FINISH

Squeeze the lemon juice over the octopus and serve with the potato salad.

SERVES 6

COOKING TIME

5 to 6 minutes

(+ 1 hour to marinate)

GRILL TEMPERATURE

Set the EGG for direct cooking.
Preheat the EGG to 390°F (200°C).

EQUIPMENT

Bamboo skewers, soaked in
water, or metal skewers

This Indonesian dish is typically prepared with goat meat, which is wrapped in papaya leaves to tenderize it. The young lamb fillets used here would be considered decadent by Indonesians but are a delicious alternative. The addition of anchovies and cucumbers to this street-food classic is a trendy update. Red onions would also be good here.

SATAY KAMBING
with anchovies and cucumbers

Ingredients

SATAY
2⅔ pounds (1.2 kg) goat or lamb fillets
2 tablespoons sunflower oil
3 cloves garlic, sliced
2 shallots, chopped
1 teaspoon shrimp paste
2 tablespoons ground cumin
2 tablespoons ground coriander
10 dried anchovies, grated
1¼ cups (300 ml) soy sauce
Juice of 2 lemons
1 tablespoon sambal (hot chili sauce)
1 teaspoon salt

CUCUMBERS
2 cucumbers
2 fresh red chiles
6 tablespoons (75 g) sugar
2 teaspoons salt
¾ cup plus 1½ tablespoons (200 ml) distilled white vinegar
Few dill sprigs

Preparation

SATAY
Cut the meat into cubes. Be careful not to cut the meat too small or it will brown too quickly and not remain pink on the inside. Thread the meat onto the skewers, spacing it evenly so it will cook uniformly. Set the skewers aside in a shallow dish. Heat the oil in a wok or frying pan over high heat on the stove top. Add the garlic, shallots, shrimp paste, cumin, and coriander and stir-fry until the shallots and garlic are light golden. Sprinkle a few of the anchovies over the top, then add the soy sauce, lemon juice, sambal, and salt and mix well. Remove from the heat and let cool. Divide the soy mixture in half and set half aside. Pour the remainder evenly over the skewers, coating the meat evenly. Marinate the meat at room temperature for 1 hour.

CUCUMBERS
Run a fork lengthwise down the sides of each cucumber to create incisions. This will allow the dressing to penetrate the skin. Halve the cucumbers lengthwise, slice crosswise, and place in a bowl.

Seed the chiles and cut lengthwise into narrow strips. Add to the cucumbers. In a small bowl, dissolve the sugar and salt in the vinegar. Pour the vinegar dressing over the cucumbers, add the dill, and toss to coat evenly.

TO FINISH
Remove the meat from the marinade and pat dry. Place the skewers on the cooking grid, close the lid of the EGG, and grill for 2 to 3 minutes on each side, until the meat is pink in the center. Remove from the EGG and sprinkle with the remaining anchovies. Serve with the remaining soy mixture and the cucumbers.

EQUIPMENT

Grill Gripper

convEGGtor

Roasting & Drip Pan

Dutch Oven or baking dish

Half Moon Cast Iron Griddle (smooth side)

GRILL TEMPERATURE

Set the EGG for direct cooking.

Preheat the EGG to 475°F (250°C).

COOKING TIME

3¾ hours

(+ overnight to marinate)

SERVES 6

PORK BELLY BACON

with sage, onion, and roasted grapes

Pork belly is inexpensive and tastes fantastic. The secret is in how it is prepared. Start this recipe the day before you plan to serve it to allow time for the seasoned meat to sit overnight and then to cook slowly. Accompany the pork belly with a salad of beans, radishes, and mint.

Ingredients

PORK BELLY

1 (3⅓-pound/1.5-kg) piece pork belly

3 tablespoons coarse sea salt

3 tablespoons fennel seeds

5 whole cloves

10 fresh bay leaves

1 large yellow onion, cut into rings

Leaves from 1 bunch sage

ROASTED GRAPES

1 bunch red grapes

Preparation

PORK BELLY

Using a sharp knife, score the pork rind in a diagonal pattern. Rub the pork with the salt and fennel seeds and insert the cloves randomly into the meat. Cover the rind side of the pork with the bay leaves and roll up tightly, with the rind facing inward. Cover and refrigerate overnight.

The next day, remove and discard the bay leaves. Place the pork belly, with the rind facing up, on the cooking grid and close the lid of the EGG. Cook for 30 minutes at 475°F (250°C), or until the rind is nice and crusty. Using the Grill Gripper, remove the grid. Place the convEGGtor, with the legs facing up, in the EGG. Add the Roasting & Drip Pan (to catch the fatty juices) and then top with the grid. Lower the temperature of the EGG to 300°F (150°C). Place the pork belly on the grid, close the lid of the EGG, and cook the pork for another

2 hours.

Place the onion rings and sage leaves in the Dutch Oven or baking dish and transfer the pork belly to the Dutch Oven, placing it on top of the onion rings. Place on the grid, close the lid of the EGG, and cook for 1 hour longer. Remove the pork from the EGG.

ROASTED GRAPES

Place the Half Moon Cast Iron Griddle, smooth side up, on the grid and close the lid of the EGG to preheat. Place the grapes on the hot Griddle, close the lid of the EGG, and roast for 12 to 15 minutes, until they start to caramelize.

TO FINISH

Cut the pork belly into slices and serve with the roasted grapes.

SERVES 6	COOKING TIME	GRILL TEMPERATURE	EQUIPMENT
	20 minutes (+ 20 minutes to cook the compote and 10 minutes for the venison to rest)	Set the EGG for direct cooking with the Cast Iron Grid. Preheat the EGG to 390°F (200°C).	Cast Iron Grid Grill Gripper convEGGtor

In the Netherlands, the combination of hunting season from May through October and fresh black currants in August creates a wonderful late-summer dish.

VENISON
with black currant compote

Ingredients

BLACK CURRANT COMPOTE

3½ tablespoons unsalted butter

1 large yellow onion, cut into thin rings

Dash of Cognac

1 pound (450 g) fresh or thawed, drained frozen black currants

1 bay leaf

Few juniper berries

Few whole cloves

1¼ cups (250 g) sugar

Few rosemary or thyme sprigs

Salt and freshly ground black pepper

1 tablespoon pink peppercorns

VENISON

2 (1-pound/450-g) boneless venison legs, at room temperature

Salt and freshly ground black pepper

Olive oil, for brushing

Salt

Preparation

BLACK CURRANT COMPOTE

Melt the butter in a frying pan over medium heat on the stop top. Add the onion and sauté for 3 to 5 minutes, until tender. Add the Cognac and deglaze the pan, stirring to dislodge any browned bits. Add the currants, bay leaf, juniper berries, cloves, sugar, and rosemary and simmer for 15 minutes, or until the currants break down. Season with salt and pepper, sprinkle with the pink peppercorns, and set aside.

VENISON

Rub the venison with salt and pepper and brush with olive oil. Place the venison on the Cast Iron Grid, close the lid of the EGG, and cook for about 5 minutes, or until browned on all sides. Transfer the venison to a plate and cover with aluminum foil to keep warm. Using the Grill Gripper, remove the Grid. Place the convEGGtor, with the legs facing up, in the EGG and replace the Grid. Place the venison back on the Grid, close the lid of the EGG, and cook for about 15 minutes, or until the venison is still very pink at the center (don't let the venison overcook). Check the meat from time to time by pressing on it (the more done it is, the more resistant it will feel).

TO FINISH

Remove the meat from the EGG, tent with aluminum foil, and let rest for 10 minutes. Cut into slices and sprinkle with salt. Serve with the black currant compote.

EQUIPMENT

Handful of cherry or other
fragrant wood chips, soaked in
water for at least 30 minutes

GRILL TEMPERATURE

Set the EGG for direct cooking
without the grid.
Preheat the EGG to 350°F (180°C).

COOKING TIME

20 to 25 minutes
(+ 1 hour to marinate)

SERVES 6

This fragrant fish is perfect for a last-minute summer gathering. It is quick to prepare on the grill, and the dish looks fantastic. It is delicious accompanied with steamed coconut rice and a spicy papaya salad.

SMOKED RED SNAPPER
with Indonesian spices, lemongrass, and lemon leaves

Ingredients

RED SNAPPER

2 (1⅔-pound/750-g) red snappers,
cleaned and scaled
6 lemongrass stalks
8 lemon leaves

INDONESIAN SPICES

2 cloves garlic
5 tablespoons (25 g) coriander seeds, crushed
1½-inch (6-cm) piece fresh turmeric, grated,
or 3 tablespoons ground turmeric
3 tablespoons ground fenugreek
Juice of 2 kaffir limes
2 tablespoons sunflower oil
Salt and freshly ground black pepper

Olive oil, for brushing
Juice of 2 lemons
Cilantro sprigs, for garnish

Preparation

RED SNAPPER

Rinse the fish under cold running water. Using a sharp knife, score a diagonal pattern into the skin on both sides of each fish.

INDONESIAN SPICES

With a mortar and pestle, mash the garlic to a pulp. Add the coriander seeds, turmeric, fenugreek, and lime juice and mix well. Stir in the sunflower oil and season with salt and pepper. Rub the fish inside and outside with the spice mixture and place the fish in a shallow dish. Tie a knot in each lemongrass stalk (so the delicious juices leak into the fish) and stuff the lemongrass and lemon leaves inside the fish. Let marinate at room temperature for 1 hour.

SMOKING AND GRILLING

Scatter the soaked wood chips over the hot coals, place the cooking grid in the EGG, and close the lid to preheat. Brush the fish with olive oil, place on the hot grid, and close the lid of the EGG. Cook the fish for 10 to 12 minutes on each side, until nicely browned.

TO FINISH

Serve the snappers whole. Squeeze the lemon juice over the top of the fish and garnish with cilantro.

GRILL TEMPERATURE

Set the EGG for indirect cooking
with the Deep Dish Pizza/Baking
Stone on the grid.
Preheat the EGG to 475°F (250°C).

EQUIPMENT

convEGGtor
Deep Dish Pizza/Baking Stone
or 14 by 2-inch (35.5 by 5-cm)
ovenproof frying pan

Known throughout Europe as a Dutch baby, this oven-baked pancake is a cross between a pancake and *clafoutis*, a French fresh fruit dessert. The typical Dutch baby is prepared with a larger quantity of eggs, which makes the pancake heavy. This puffed version is much lighter and a good choice for breakfast or makes a wonderful dessert with a scoop of ice cream. Make sure the Deep Dish Pizza/Baking Stone is hot when you add the batter, so the edges of the pancake will puff nicely.

PUFFED PANCAKE
with peaches and plum compote

Ingredients

PANCAKE BATTER
2½ cups (315 g) all-purpose flour, or 1¼ cups (150 g) each all-purpose flour and whole wheat flour
4 eggs
1⅓ cups (315 ml) whole milk
Grated zest of 1 lemon
4 tablespoons sugar
1 teaspoon vanilla extract

PLUM COMPOTE
6 plums, halved and pitted
1 tablespoon ground cardamom
1 cinnamon stick
2 tablespoons sugar

4 tablespoons unsalted butter
2 peaches, halved, pitted, and sliced
Crème fraîche, for topping
Ground cinnamon, for sprinkling
Confectioners' sugar, for dusting

Preparation

PANCAKE BATTER
Sift the flour into a big bowl. Form a well in the center of the flour and break the eggs into the well. Whisk together the flour and eggs, then add the milk in a slow, steady stream while whisking constantly. Continue stirring until the batter is smooth. Whisk in the lemon zest, sugar, and vanilla. Let the batter rest for 30 minutes.

PLUM COPOTE
Place the plums, cardamom, cinnamon stick, and sugar in a small saucepan over low heat on the stove top. Cook, stirring occasionally, for about 10 minutes, or until the plums have softened. Set aside.

BAKING THE PANCAKE
Add the butter to the hot Deep Dish Pizza/Baking Stone or ovenproof frying pan and close the lid of the EGG just until the butter is hot. Open the lid, arrange the sliced peaches in the Deep Dish Stone, and pour the batter on top. Close the lid and bake the pancake for 20 to 25 minutes, until lightly browned and the edges puff.

TO FINISH
Scoop the reserved plum compote and the crème fraîche on top of the pancake. Sprinkle with cinnamon, dust with confectioners' sugar, and serve immediately.

GRILLED RICOTTA

with almonds, figs, and sherry

Ricotta is a very mild cheese that can be served in a variety of ways. In this recipe, it is grilled alongside fresh figs and almonds, and a spiced, syrupy dry sherry is drizzled over the top.

Ingredients

RICOTTA
1 (10 to 12-ounce/280 to 340-g) whole-milk ricotta cheese in a basket, unmolded

SYRUPY SHERRY
1 tablespoon fennel seeds
1 tablespoon coriander seeds
Small handful of star anise pods
1 cup (240 ml) dry sherry, preferably Spanish

ALMONDS AND FIGS
¾ cup (100 g) almonds
12 ripe figs, halved lengthwise

Preparation

RICOTTA
Place the ricotta on the Half Moon Cast Iron Griddle and close the lid of the EGG. Grill the ricotta for about 25 minutes, or until light brown.

SYRUPY SHERRY
While the ricotta cooks, combine the fennel seeds, coriander seeds, star anise, and sherry in a small saucepan over low heat on the stove top and heat gently to meld the flavors and to reduce slightly.

ALMONDS AND FIGS
Place the almonds in the small frying pan, place on the cooking grid alongside the ricotta, close the lid of the EGG, and cook, stirring and checking occasionally, until toasted. This will take only a few minutes. During the last 10 minutes of cooking the ricotta, add the figs, cut side up, to the Griddle.

Transfer the ricotta to a serving platter and arrange the figs and almonds alongside. Pour the sherry and spices over the ricotta.

BIG GREEN EGG BIG CHEFS

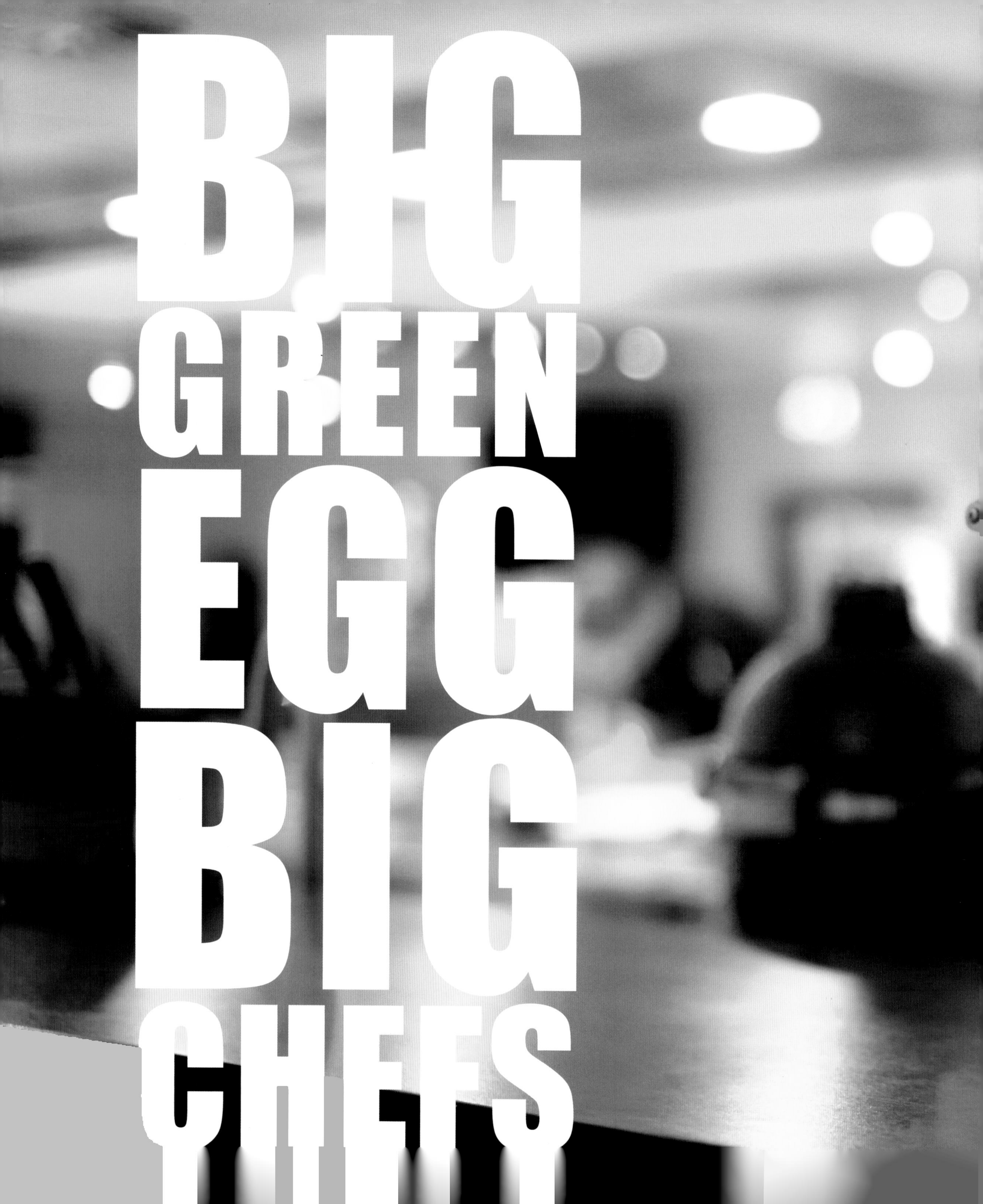

what do you prepare FOR THE BEST CHEF in the world?

Leonard Elenbaas

Pure Passie

There was a moment of hesitation when Leonard Elenbaas received a phone call asking him to give a cooking demonstration using the Big Green Egg at chef René Redzepi's award-winning Noma restaurant in Copenhagen. "Luckily I had only a few days before the event, so I didn't even have time to get nervous," recalls the chef from Pure Passie restaurant. "What do you prepare for the best chef in the world?" Wessel Buddingh, director of the Big Green Egg in Europe, had asked Elenbaas to do demonstrations in the past. But this was different. Elenbaas continues, "I got *côte de boeuf* from the butcher Piet van de Berg. I also had ingredients for preparing bread with me. And all this had to go through customs."

Once in Copenhagen, there were three Big Green Eggs ready for use. "I prepared dough while the other chefs from Noma drifted in. They introduced themselves and quickly we were all at ease and work. All the chefs had their foods to prepare on the Big Green Egg: produce, bread, red meat, bear meat, fish, and shellfish—we tried everything. It was wonderful to practice with top-notch chefs. We tried such things as moss for smoking celery root, and we smoked foods with hazelnuts. Next, we increased the heat to 750°F (400°C) to grill red cabbage. The underside of the cabbage was charred, but the top stayed tender. Then we placed the grilled cabbage into a juicer to enhance the flavor of the other ingredients, creating juice that became raw cooked cabbage." Cabbage squared. As thanks for his successful mission, chef Elenbaas received a bag of juniper berry–flavored wood chips.

You can call chef Elenbaas a Big Green Egg ambassador because he prepares a special menu, from appetizer to main course to dessert, using only the EGG. "The beauty of the Big Green Egg is that everything cooks very evenly. That's because of its egg shape. Even baking bread or cakes works very well." The EGG fits well with Elenbaas's concept of being in charge of everything: there are no unnecessary purchases, and he creates all of his own dishes.

"We are sitting here in southern Holland surrounded by growers, two of whom grow especially for our restaurant: special vegetables, fruits, herbs, and edible flowers. The vegetables come out of the ground in the morning and at night they are on the menu and on your plate. It's better to leave the cauliflower in the ground another night than to have it sit in the refrigerator for a night, where it will lose flavor and vitamins." Daikon and other sometimes forgotten vegetables are used in delightful ways by Elenbaas. "If you puff a sweet potato in the Big Green Egg, the sugars will caramelize and make the potato even sweeter. Add the barbecue flavor and you have something no other kitchen equipment can give you." Local hunters deliver geese, rabbits, doves, and ducks. Anglers bring freshly caught fish. (The restaurant is close to Hoek van Holland, a notable fishing locale.) Together with an organic farm, Elenbaas makes his own cheese, such as a special varietal arugula. He also serves locally produced Maas Rijn Ijsel veal, using all the body parts, including the brain.

If you had told Elenbaas ten years ago that he would have his own restaurant and that it would be listed in a Michelin Guide, he would have laughed in your face. At that time, he was in the infantry in Curaçao. His love of cooking was already instilled; he prepared food at local eateries. But when he returned to Holland, he decided to take his hobby seriously and enrolled in a private cooking school. "My self-discipline from my days in the military served me well," he says, describing how he simultaneously worked hard during the day and studied equally hard in the evenings. He learned his trade in a star-rated restaurant "cooking supertight and presenting plates perfectly." But it wasn't what he aspired to. "Pleasure is paramount. When my wife, Claudia, and I were given the chance to take over my father-in-law's restaurant, we jumped at it. Who doesn't want to be a chef at his own restaurant?" Elenbaas remodeled the restaurant in just three months. In the beginning, he continued to serve pork and cream sauce, but the menu eventually grew increasingly more sophisticated, becoming the thriving restaurant that Pure Passie is today.

Tip: Never use charcoal briquettes. They are filled with chemicals and give off a chemical smoke that leaves an unpleasant taste. They also create residue and ashes that prevent airflow, so the Big Green Egg will not work properly. There are many types of wood chips available, each with its own unique flavor, such as cherry or chips made from whiskey barrels. Adding wood chips to your coals will provide an extra taste dimension to your dishes.

Aromatic smoking woods are a very desirable and popular form of seasoning, adding a new dimension of flavor to foods without adding a single calorie or gram of fat. Think of smoking woods as seasonings; just as each herb or spice in our spice rack imparts a different flavor to foods, each variety of wood, from apple to mesquite to hickory and beyond, infuses food with its unique flavor.

www.biggreenegg.com

EQUIPMENT

Handful of wood chips (such as
whiskey barrel–flavored), soaked
in water for at least 30 minutes
convEGGtor
Roasting & Drip Pan
Cast Iron Grid
Baking dish

GRILL TEMPERATURE

Set the EGG for indirect cooking
with the convEGGtor.
Preheat the EGG to 250°F (120°C).

COOKING TIME

5½ hours
(+ 2 months to make the syrup, overnight to marinate the
pork belly, and 20 to 30 minutes to cook the celery root)

SERVES 4

GOOSE LIVERS AND
smoked pork belly with celery root sauce, parsnip chips, and pine tops syrup

Ingredients

YOUNG PINE TOPS SYRUP

Handful of young pine tops (to fill a canning jar)
1 part granulated sugar
1 part dark brown sugar

SMOKED PORK BELLY

5 cups (1.2 L) water
¾ cup (100 g) sea salt
4 tablespoons sugar
4 juniper berries
4 black peppercorns
1 bay leaf
3 cloves garlic
3 rosemary sprigs
1 (10½-ounce/300-g) piece pork belly

CELERY ROOT SAUCE

1 (1-pound/450-g) celery root, peeled and diced
½ cup (120 ml) heavy cream
½ cup (120 ml) whole milk
Salt and freshly ground black pepper

PATTYPAN SQUASH AND CARROTS

1 small patty pan squash
8 to 12 mini carrots
1½ tablespoons unsalted butter
1 basil sprig, chopped

PARSNIP CHIPS

1 parsnip
1 tablespoon vegetable oil
Salt

GOOSE LIVER

4 (2¾-ounce/80-g) goose livers, frozen
Salt and freshly ground black pepper

Preparation

YOUNG PINE TOPS SYRUP

In June, the pine trees are full of young, green shoots.
Cut and place them in a canning jar and cover them
with the granulated and brown sugars. Allow the pine
sugar to set for 2 months. After 2 months, pass the sugar
through a fine-mesh sieve into a small saucepan. Cook
on the stove top at 225°F (110°C) until a tasty brown
syrup forms. Run the syrup through a fine-mesh sieve
and transfer to a squeeze bottle.

SMOKED PORK BELLY

Combine the water, salt, sugar, juniper berries, peppercorns, bay leaf, garlic, and rosemary in a medium saucepan
over medium-high heat on the stove top and heat, stirring,
until the salt and sugar dissolve. Let the marinade cool.
Combine the pork belly and marinade in a lock-top plastic
bag and marinate in the refrigerator overnight.

The next day, scatter the wood chips over the hot coals.
Place the convEGGtor, with the legs facing up, in the
EGG, top with the Roasting & Drip Pan and then with the
Cast Iron Grid, and close the lid of the EGG to preheat.
Place the pork belly on the hot Grid, close the lid of the
EGG, and smoke the meat for 5 hours. Let the pork cool
for a while before slicing.

CELERY ROOT SAUCE

Combine the celery root with water to cover in a
medium saucepan, bring to a boil on the stove top, and
boil for 20 to 30 minutes, until tender when pierced with
a knife tip. Drain well, transfer to a blender, and purée until
smooth and thick. Pass the purée through a fine-mesh sieve
to remove any fibers, then transfer to a clean saucepan. Add
the cream and milk, place over medium heat on the stove
top, and heat until warm. Season with salt and pepper. The
sauce should be thick and creamy. Just before using, reheat
gently until warm and transfer to a squeeze bottle.

PATTYPAN SQUASH AND CARROTS

Cut the pattypan squash into chunks. Scrub the carrots
but do not peel. Bring a medium saucepan filled with
water to a boil on the stove top, add the squash and
carrots, and blanch briefly. Drain well. Melt the butter
in a small frying on the stove top over medium heat,
add the squash, carrots, and basil, and cook lightly.

PARSNIP CHIPS

Using a vegetable peeler, peel the parsnip, then cut
it lengthwise into long, thin strips. Rinse the parsnip
strips with water and pat dry. Heat the oil in a small
frying pan over medium heat on the stove top,
add the parsnip strips, and fry briefly until lightly
browned. Transfer the strips to a paper towel to
drain, then sprinkle with salt.

GOOSE LIVER

Carefully remove the convEGGtor. Increase the
temperature of the EGG to 475°F (240°C) and
preheat the Cast Iron Grid. Put the livers on the Grid,
close the lid of the EGG, and cook the livers for 30
seconds on each side. Remove the livers from the
EGG. Lower the temperature of the EGG to 265°F
(130°C). Place the livers in the baking dish, place the
dish in the EGG, close the lid of the EGG, and cook
the livers for 8 minutes, until just done. Season with
salt and pepper.

TO FINISH

Place a portion of pork belly and goose liver on each
plate. Top with the squash, carrots, and parsnip chips.
Squeeze drops of the pine syrup and celery root
sauce around each plate.

MAKES 1 LOAF	COOKING TIME	GRILL TEMPERATURE	EQUIPMENT
	50 minutes	Set the EGG for indirect cooking.	convEGGtor
	(+ 18 hours for the dough to rise)	Preheat the EGG to 425°F (220°C).	Dutch Oven

Bread that doesn't require kneading saves time and is easier to digest because fewer gluten molecules are released. The dough is wetter than traditional bread dough, which allows the gluten molecules to move around and develop more easily. The wetter dough and gentler handling also preserves the pockets of gas from the yeast fermentation better than traditionally kneaded bread dough. During the lengthy rising process, the bread develops a slightly acidic taste. Baker Jan Bronswijk learned this method in the United States and perfected the recipe. Chef Leonard Elenbaas then refined the method using the Big Green Egg and now offers bread-baking workshops.

no knead BREAD

Ingredients

7 cups (830 g) nine-grain flour, plus flour for sprinkling
1 tablespoon plus 2 teaspoons salt
1¾ teaspoons active dry yeast
2¾ cups (650 ml) water
Vegetable oil, for oiling

Preparation

Combine the flour, salt, yeast, and water in a large bowl and stir with a wooden spoon until a dough forms. Cover the bowl with plastic wrap and let the dough rise at room temperature for 16 hours. Sprinkle a clean work surface liberally with flour. Turn the dough out onto the surface and fold in half. Then form the dough into a ball by stretching and tucking the edges of the dough underneath the ball. Flour a large bowl, place the dough ball, fold side up, in the flour-coated bowl, and cover the bowl with plastic wrap. Let the dough rise for another 2 hours at room temperature.

Lightly oil the bottom and sides of the Dutch Oven and place in the closed EGG to preheat. Place the dough in the Dutch Oven, cover the Dutch Oven with its lid, and close the lid of the EGG. Bake the bread for 30 minutes. Remove the lid of the Dutch Oven, close the lid of the EGG, and bake for 20 minutes longer.

TO FINISH
Let the bread rest for a short time before slicing and serving.

COOKING TIME

65 minutes
(+ 1 day to drain the yogurt, 1½ hours for
the dough to rise, and 1 hour to bake the
meringues)

GRILL TEMPERATURE

Preheat to 425°F (220°C).
Set the EGG for indirect cooking
with the Pizza & Baking Stone on
the grid.

EQUIPMENT

convEGGtor
Pizza & Baking Stone
12 ovenproof baba au rhum molds (at least 2 inches/
5 cm deep and 2 to 3 inches/5 to 7.5 cm in diameter)
Baking dish
Grill Gripper
Cast Iron Grid

The Big Green Egg gives this classic dessert an
unusual and intriguing slightly smoky flavor.

BABA AU RHUM
and grilled-banana ice cream and pink meringue cookies

Ingredients

CURD

4¼ cups (1 kg) plain yogurt
2 teaspoons vanilla extract
Honey, for sweetening

BABA AU RHUM

3½ tablespoons (40 g) sugar
¾ cup (180 ml) warm water
1¾ teaspoons active dry yeast
2⅔ cups (335 g) all-purpose flour
2½ teaspoons salt
¾ cup (180 ml) eggs (about 4 eggs)
⅔ cup (150 g) unsalted butter, melted and cooled
½ cup (75 g) rum-soaked raisins

RUM MIXTURE

1½ cups (360 ml) rum
1½ cups (360 ml) water
1½ cups (300 g) sugar

APPLE COMPOTE

3 Jonagold apples, peeled and diced
Jelly sugar, as needed

PINK MERINGUES

2½ cups (300 g) confectioners' sugar
¾ cup (180 ml) pasteurized egg whites,
or 7 fresh egg whites
Rose petal sugar, as needed to color (optional)

GRILLED-BANANA ICE CREAM

12 bananas (to yield about 4½ cups/1 kg
puréed)
3 cups (680 ml) sugar water (made with
equal parts sugar and water)
⅓ cup (80 ml) fresh lemon juice
1¼ cups (300 ml) water

Red currants, for garnish

Preparation

CURD

Line a large sieve with cheesecloth, place over a
bowl, and spoon the yogurt into the sieve. Let drain
in the refrigerator for 1 day. Add the vanilla and
sweeten with honey. Refrigerate until serving.

BABA AU RHUM

Whisk together the sugar and warm water in a
small bowl until the sugar dissolves, then stir in
the yeast and let stand for 5 to 10 minutes, until
foamy. In a large bowl, sift together the flour and
salt; make a well in center of the flour mixture and
add the eggs, yeast mixture, and butter to the well.
Using a wooden spoon and then your hands, gradually work the flour mixture into the egg mixture
until a dough forms. Add the raisins and work them
into the dough until evenly distributed. Continue
to knead the dough in the bowl until it is soft and
smooth. Form the dough into 12 small mounds,
each weighing about 2 ounces (55 g). Spray the
baba au rhum molds with nonstick cooking spray,

then dust each mold with flour. Place a dough
mound in each mold. Set the molds in a warm spot
and let the dough rise for about 1½ hours, or until
doubled in size.

Place the molds on the hot Pizza & Baking Stone,
close the lid of the EGG, and bake for about
25 minutes, or until golden brown.

RUM MIXTURE

Just before the babas are ready, combine the rum,
water, and sugar in a small saucepan over high
heat on the stove top and bring to a boil, stirring to
dissolve the sugar. Boil for about 5 minutes, until
a light syrup forms.

Unmold the warm babas and place in a shallow
baking dish. Slowly drizzle the rum mixture over
the babas, allowing it to soak in.

APPLE COMPOTE

Carefully remove the Pizza & Baking Stone from
the EGG. Lower the heat in the EGG to 300°F
(150°C). Place the apples in the baking dish, place
the dish on the cooking grid, close the lid of the
EGG, and cook for 15 minutes. Pour the apples into
a fine-mesh sieve, capturing the liquid in a small
saucepan. Set the apples aside in a small heatproof
bowl. Following the package directions, add the
jelly sugar to the apple liquid. Place the pan over
high heat on the stove top and bring to a rolling
boil. Pour over the reserved apples and let cool in
the refrigerator.

PINK MERINGUES

Preheat the oven to 200°F (100°C). Line a baking sheet with parchment paper. In a medium bowl, whisk together the confectioners' sugar and egg whites until the mixture is light, yet firm, then whisk in just enough rose petal sugar to color lightly. Spoon the mixture into a pastry bag fitted with a fluted tip and pipe into small mounds onto the baking sheet. Place in the oven to dry for 1 hour.

GRILLED-BANANA ICE CREAM

Using the Grill Gripper, remove the cooking grid from the EGG. Place the Cast Iron Grid in the EGG, increase the heat to 390°F (200°C), and close the lid to preheat. Place the bananas on the hot Grid, close the lid of the EGG, and cook the bananas for 12 minutes on each side. Remove the bananas from the EGG, remove the skins, and purée the bananas in a blender. Combine the banana purée, sugar water, lemon juice, and water

in a bowl and mix well. Transfer the mixture to an ice cream maker and freeze for 8 minutes (or according to the manufacturer's directions), or until a light, airy ice cream forms.

TO FINISH

Place a baba au rhum, a portion of the ice cream, and a scoop of the curd on each plate and alternate the apple compote and meringues in a line alongside. Garnish with the red currants.

I'M SUCH A know-it-all, I'M BETTER off being my OWN BOSS

Dave De Belder
De Godevaart

The Belgian media have called him the "culinary hope" of Antwerp because six years ago he introduced the port city to the molecular kitchen (a "playful kitchen," according to the chef). Chef Dave De Belder continues to reinvent himself at De Godevaart, his restaurant housed in the storefront of a former fish market on the Sint-Katelijnevest.

A self-described culinary globetrotter, De Belder explains that he got his wanderlust from his father. "My father was a top chef for Holland America. For my entire youth, I was shuttled between Antwerp and Brussels. My uncle was a chef at a Hilton, so this lifestyle was spoon-fed to me. When I was young, being a chef was not yet my life's goal, as cooking was not cool at school."

At sixteen, however, De Belder followed in his father's footsteps, taking a job in the galley on a boat. But "my gastronomical revelation—my heaven—came at De Librije [a restaurant in the Netherlands]. Jonnie Boer is the champ! I attended a culinary program in Belgium, but I completed my internship with Jonnie Boer, Robert Kranenborg, and Ron Blaauw, where I really learned my trade. In Belgium, I was surrounded primarily by classic kitchens. My dad prompted me to look around in the Netherlands because, according to him, that was where it was happening. He was right. The Belgian culinary world is very old-fashioned." De Belder later interned at the world-famous elBulli in Spain, which closed in 2011.

He was relatively young when he opened his own business. "I'm so cocky; I think it's better to be your own boss." De Godevaart opened shortly before the financial crisis. "We were knocked about some, but we survived. We made the kitchen accessible in a timely manner. We stopped using linen tablecloths and menus that cost 200 euros. Who can pay for that anymore? I can still serve the same langoustines, caviar, or foie gras prepared in three-star restaurants, but I will never make that money back. Ideally, perfection remains my goal, but the financial crisis really woke me up. In the beginning, I served ten courses from which people could choose their selections. I would stand in the kitchen for up to two hours preparing main courses only. That was definitely a wake-up call. Now, I have more experience. I have been here for six years and know better what the Dave De Belder style entails.

"My wife, Tamara, and I wanted to create a statement in Antwerp because here you can easily find tourist traps and poor-quality restaurants. We offer a purely innovative kitchen that revolves around a pure dining experience. At our restaurant, you will be served a plate of food, not a main course using ten different techniques. I am going for a melding of tastes that are carried out in absolute perfection, which is how I measure success. People do not want twenty different flavors on their plate or three hundred different garnishes. On the other hand, I do not participate in the gastro-pub trend known as Nouveau Ruig." (This refers to getting back to basics in both presentation and foods served at eating establishments; no expensive bottled water or fancy tablecloths but rather locally produced foods at reasonable prices—in other words, no frills.) In De Belder's search for reinvention, he looks to new techniques as a "distillation and fermentation process."

De Belder prefers to serve local products. "I have difficulty with flying in tuna from five thousand miles away so it can be eaten raw." However, local is not an end in itself, so the fish comes from Rotterdam and the meat from Piet van den Berg (a 120-year-old Dutch meat company). "The Dutch are better business people and more focused on the presentation.

"I learned about the Big Green Egg from Jonnie Boer. No one was using the EGG, and I wanted one the minute I opened my own kitchen. My restaurant was the first one in Antwerp to use it. At Christmas, I even gave them to the guys in the kitchen. At home, it is also an unbelievable tool. Why? You can use it as a smoker, bake with it, barbecue, all in your own backyard. Grill and smoke delicious fish, who doesn't want that? The EGG is the Bentley of devices."

At De Godevaart, the dove recipe on page 140 is prepared with celery, pumpkin, macadamia, heart, liver, and coffee. "First, we braise the birds and then remove the innards, which are also braised. We grill the doves for six minutes at 340°F [170°C], let them rest, and the meat comes right off the bone. A little tap, the dove is done. We serve the heart and liver in a very classic manner, baked with garlic and rosemary, similar to how they were served in France one hundred years ago."

Tip: "It important to learn to light and to regulate the temperature of the EGG. When lighting the EGG, give it enough oxygen so it lights faster. For extra flavor, use wood chips soaked in Jack Daniels whiskey. "

www.degodevaart.be

COOKING TIME

12 hours

(+ 4 days to pickle and

24 hours to cool the neck)

GRILL TEMPERATURE

Set the EGG for indirect cooking.

Preheat the EGG to 200°F (100°C).

EQUIPMENT

convEGGtor

Stainless steel or other nonreactive roasting pan

The biggest mistake you can make with the Big Green Egg is to fire it up too high. Learn to experiment with and regulate the temperature of the Big Green Egg to create a delicious meal every time you grill.

PICKLED PIG'S NECK
with saffron aioli and
MUSTARD JUS

Ingredients

PIG'S NECK
12½ cups (3 L) water
2¾ cups (380 g) pickling salt
1 (3-pound/1.3-kg) boneless pig's neck (boned by your butcher)
Sunflower oil, for cooking neck
Few rosemary sprigs
Few cloves garlic
Few bay leaves

SAFFRON AIOLI
2 eggs, at room temperature
1 tablespoon sushi vinegar
1 teaspoon salt
2 cloves garlic, finely minced
Pinch of saffron threads, soaked in 1 tablespoon water
1 teaspoon cayenne pepper
1 cup (240 ml) sunflower oil

MUSTARD JUS
2 cups (480 ml) chicken stock
4 tablespoons coarse-grain mustard
½ cup (100 g) yellow mustard

Cabbage leaves, for garnish
Sorrel leaves, for garnish
Marigold petals, for garnish

Preparation

PIG'S NECK
Pour the water into a container large enough to accommodate the pig's neck, add the pickling salt, and stir to dissolve the salt. Add the neck (it should be submerged in the liquid), cover tightly, and refrigerate for 4 days.

When ready to cook, preheat the EGG for indirect cooking as directed. Remove the pig's neck from the brine and pat dry. Lightly coat the bottom of the stainless steel roasting pan with the oil, then add the rosemary, garlic, bay leaves, and the neck. Place the pan in the EGG, close the lid of the EGG, and cook the neck for 12 hours, or until very tender. Remove the neck from the EGG, transfer to a clean container, let cool down a bit, cover, and refrigerate for at least 24 hours.

Preheat the EGG for indirect cooking to 390°F (200°C). Remove the neck from the refrigerator and cut into thick slices. Place the slices on the cooking grid, close the lid of the EGG, and cook for a few minutes on each side, until the slices are crispy.

SAFFRON AIOLI
In a food processor or blender, combine the eggs, vinegar, salt, garlic, saffron and water, and cayenne pepper and process until well blended. With the machine running continuously, add the oil in a very fine, slow stream and process until the mixture is thick and smooth. (Once an emulsion has formed, the oil can be added a little more quickly.)

MUSTARD JUS
Combine the stock and both mustards in a small saucepan over medium heat on the stove top and heat, stirring occasionally, until warm.

TO FINISH
Serve the pig neck slices with the saffron aioli and drizzle the mustard jus around the plate. Garnish with cabbage and sorrel leaves and marigold petals.

EQUIPMENT

Handful of apple or other fragrant wood chips, soaked in water for at least 30 minutes (optional)

Cast Iron Grid

GRILL TEMPERATURE

Set the EGG for direct cooking without the grid.

Preheat the EGG to 350°F (180°C).

COOKING TIME

55 minutes

(+ 20 to 30 minutes to cook the celery root and 5 minutes to cook the mushrooms)

SERVES 4

DOVE
with celery root, sweet-sour
PUMPKIN
and chanterelles

Serve this dish with a pinot noir that is full and soft, with lots of spicy red fruit. For example, a Spätburgunder from Germany will complement its flavors beautifully.

Ingredients

DOVES

4 (1¼-pound/570-g) young doves, cleaned

Salt and freshly ground black pepper

Clarified butter, for rubbing

⅓ to ½ cup (40 to 55 g) finely chopped macadamia nuts

CREAMED CELERY ROOT

1 small celery root, peeled and diced

1¼ cups (300 ml) whole milk

2 tablespoons unsalted butter

Salt

PUMPKIN BALLS

1 (2¼-pound/1-kg) pumpkin

7 tablespoons (100 g) unsalted butter

Salt

1 part water

1 part distilled white vinegar

1 part sugar

CHANTERELLES

Clarified butter, for sautéing

3½ ounces (100 g) small chanterelles or a mix of small wild mushrooms, cleaned

Salt and freshly ground black pepper

Preparation

DOVES

Scatter the soaked wood chips over the hot coals. Place the Cast Iron Grid in the EGG and close the lid to preheat. Season the doves with salt and pepper, rub them with the clarified butter, and place them on the hot Grid. Close the lid of the EGG and cook the birds for 6 to 9 minutes, until their breasts turn pink. Remove the doves from the EGG and let them rest. Slice off the breasts, saving the wings and legs for another dish, or let the legs cook a little longer in the closed EGG and serve alongside the breasts. Coat the top of each breast with the macadamia nuts.

CREAMED CELERY ROOT

Combine the celery root, milk, butter, and salt in a saucepan over medium heat on the stove top, bring to a simmer, and cook for 20 to 30 minutes, until the celery root is soft. Remove from the heat and, using an immersion blender or a stand blender, purée the celery root mixture until creamy.

PUMPKIN BALLS

Lower the temperature in the EGG to 320°F (160°C). Place the whole pumpkin on the Cast Iron Grid, close the lid of the EGG, and cook for 45 minutes, or until the pumpkin is tender when pierced with a knife. Remove the pumpkin from the EGG, let cool until it can be handled, then halve, seed, and peel it. Cut into chunks and, using the immersion blender or the stand blender, purée the pumpkin with the butter and with salt to taste. Using a melon baller, scoop the purée into small half balls and place in a bowl.

Combine equal parts water, vinegar, and sugar in a medium saucepan and bring to a boil over high heat on the stove top, stirring to dissolve the sugar. Pour the mixture over the pumpkin half balls, immersing them. Let cool, then cover and refrigerate.

CHANTERELLES

Heat a little clarified butter in a frying pan over medium heat on the stove top. Add the chanterelles and sauté for about 5 minutes, until lightly browned.

TO FINISH

Spoon some creamed celery root on each plate. Top with the dove breasts. Arrange the pumpkin half balls and the mushrooms around the breasts.

TIME FOR THE CULINARY SNACK ON THE STREET. ARE YOU HUNGRY? BOOM

Sjaak Borsboom, Olivier van der Ree, and Jeroen Simons

Gastrovan

There are only three pesky things in life: barking dogs, snoring pigs, and the Gastrovan moving on. Three chefs had a childhood dream to explore the world with a gastronomical food cart—and they succeeded. Last year, they traveled from Zeeland via France to Galicia. Along the way, the three pilgrims, chefs Sjaak, Olivier, and Jeroen, asked local growers about their regional fare and then proceeded to prepare these same meals for those growers and their families. The chefs created a feast based on classic recipes, such as *cassoulet de Toulouse* or *pollo a la vasca*. *Gastrovan*, their cookbook, was a result of their experiences on the road. The caravan was temporarily in Vlissingen, where the trio stopped at the restaurant Zeeuwen in De Timmerfabriek to prepare potatoes, crabs, and oysters. During their journey, they also ran a pop-up restaurant in public trains traveling throughout the Netherlands, and Theater de Veste in Delft asked them to provide guests with an ad hoc menu for a few months. At last word, they were heading to Italy for more culinary adventure and fun.

An old rectory serves as their base when they are home in the Netherlands. De Gastrovan, a 1985 Fiat Arca, stands ready to serve customers. Two enormous Hungarian Mangalitsa pigs, named Worst and Onrust, are typically scurrying around in the garden. The medium-size, long-haired brown beasts regularly uproot the tiles in the abandoned garden in search of acorns and carrots.

Chef Saajak started the Gastrovan threesome. He worked as a chef in a restaurant in the Netherlands when, "One day I was standing there with these beautiful, fresh ingredients in my hands and thinking, 'I don't have any idea where these came from.' I decided to find out." Chef Jeroen adds: "Sjaak called me and Olivier over. We wanted to make contact with everyday people during our search and decided to build a kitchen in the Gastrovan. Luckily, chef Olivier did two years of technical studies at the university, which came in handy." Chef Sjaak adds, "Even when I was a young boy, I wanted to cook. I have been pursuing it since I was nine years old. Cooking connected me with people, sharing something of myself with the person I was cooking for. I love the social aspect and the ongoing contact with others. Most chefs never talk with their guests. But we love feedback."

Chef Jeroen has especially fond memories of the wholesale suppliers he has met. "You can learn a lot from them, all about wine, produce, meat, fish, you name it. Briny soil, different kinds of grass—everything influences what you eat. These are people with passion. What you learn makes you look differently at a piece of meat—it makes you look at it with the same love as the producer." Among other things, chef Sjaak learned why the beef in beef bourguignonne is braised in a local variety of pinot noir: "The tannins make the meat tender."

Gastrovan is not unique to the Netherlands. More and more rolling kitchens are seen throughout the region. The chefs think that's great. Chef Jeroen says, "You can start with a minimum investment. A small refrigerator, a countertop, two burners, and you can cut loose. It forces you to prepare simple, fresh meals. Isn't it a bit crazy to find Vietnamese spring rolls or some French fries only in food carts? Time for a culinary snack. Are you hungry? Boom. Surprise yourself with something contemporary."

For now, the Gastrovan crew is using ingredients from the Netherlands: escargots, lovely cheeses and other dairy products, fish from Scheveningen, and farm-raised eel. They say that they cook with the Big Green Egg more and more because they love to grill. "It's an instinct we like to admit to," says chef Sjaak. Chef Jeroen explains, "If you have a first-rate piece of meat and add the grill flavor to it, it complements the meat taste beautifully. Besides, it's an excuse to start a fire. There is nothing more beautiful than preparing food on an open fire. Becoming the boss of the flames. The Big Green Egg makes that easier."

Tip from chef Jeroen Simons: Give the Big Green Egg time. If you want to move toward 195°F (90°C), don't push it too much. Give the EGG time to stabilize. It is not a gas stove.

www.gastrovan.nl

EQUIPMENT
Springform pan
Round Roasting & Drip Pan

GRILL TEMPERATURE
Set the EGG for direct cooking.
Preheat the EGG to 300°F (150°C).

COOKING TIME
12 minutes
(+ 1½ hours to bake the cake,
6 hours to freeze the cake, and
12 minutes to toast the nuts)

SERVES 10

ice cream CAKE
with whipped cream and blackberries

This cake looks like an igloo! The inside has homemade ice cream surrounded by almond cake, and the outside is made of meringue. The cake protects the ice cream while the meringue cooks and gives the dessert a nostalgic "marshmallow" flavor. The warm-cold contrast of this dish is particularly wonderful.

Ingredients

ICE CREAM
3¾ cups (500 g) hazelnuts
4¼ cups (1 L) whole milk
1 strip lemon peel
⅔ cup (160 g) egg yolks (8 to 9 yolks)
1 cup plus 1 tablespoon (225 g) sugar

ALMOND CAKE
2 cups (250 g) all-purpose flour
3⅔ cups (350 g) almond flour
Pinch of salt
6 eggs
1⅓ cups (300 g) unsalted butter, at room temperature
1¼ cups (250 g) sugar
2 teaspoons grated orange zest
Scant ¾ cup (200 ml) amaretto

MERINGUE
4 egg whites
1⅓ cups (280 g) sugar

TO FINISH
1¼ cups (300 ml) heavy cream
4 tablespoons sugar
Reserved ¾ cup (100 g) toasted hazelnuts
1⅓ cups (200 g) fresh blackberries

Preparation

ICE CREAM
Preheat the oven to 325°F (165°C). Spread the hazelnuts on a rimmed baking sheet, place in the oven, and toast for 10 to 12 minutes, until they take on color and are fragrant. Transfer the warm nuts to a kitchen towel and rub vigorously to remove the skins. Set aside 2 cups (265 g) of the hazelnuts for adding to the ice cream later and set aside ¾ cup (100 g) for garnishing the finished cake. Transfer the remaining 1 cup (135 g) hazelnuts to a food processor, add 1 tablespoon of the milk, and process until an oil-like substance forms. Set aside.

Combine the remaining milk and the lemon peel in a medium saucepan over medium heat on the stove top and heat until small bubbles appear along the edges of the pan. Meanwhile, in a medium bowl, whisk together the egg yolks and sugar until pale yellow. Remove and discard the lemon peel from the hot milk, then slowly add the hot milk to the egg yolk mixture while whisking constantly. Return the mixture to the saucepan and place over low heat on the stove top. Heat, stirring constantly, until the temperature reaches 180°F (83°C). Stir in the reserved hazelnut-milk mixture, remove from the heat, pour into a clean medium bowl, and let cool completely. (Use an ice-water bath or refrigerate the bowl to speed the cooling.) Pour the custard into an ice cream maker and freeze according to the manufacturer's directions. Crush the reserved 2 cups (265 g) toasted hazelnuts, add to the ice cream, and churn a few more times to

distribute evenly. Transfer the ice cream to an airtight container and place in the freezer until needed.

ALMOND CAKE
Preheat the oven to 325°F (165°C). Butter a 9-inch (23-cm) springform pan. Sift the all-purpose flour into a medium bowl. Add the almond flour and salt and whisk briefly to mix. In a separate bowl, whisk together the eggs until blended. In a large bowl, using a handheld mixer, beat together the butter and sugar on medium speed until light and fluffy. On low speed, add the flour mixture in three batches alternately with the egg mixture in two batches, beginning and ending with the flour mixture and beating until combined after each addition. Beat in the orange zest.

Pour the batter into the prepared pan and bake for about 1½ hours, or until a skewer inserted into the center comes out clean. Let cool completely in the pan on a wire rack. Turn the cake out of the pan and slice it in half horizontally to make 2 layers (makes enough for 2 ice cream cakes).

BUILDING THE CAKE
Cut the cake into slices about ⅓ inch (8 mm) thick. Line a bowl 8 inches (20 cm) in diameter with plastic wrap, allowing the edges to hang over the sides. Then line the bowl with the cake slices until it resembles an upside-down igloo. Evenly sprinkle the cake in the bowl with some of the amaretto. Fill the lined bowl with one-fourth of the ice cream, then cover

the ice cream completely with more cake slices and press down gently with your hands to ensure the cake adheres to the ice cream. Sprinkle the cake with the remaining amaretto. Bring the overhanging plastic wrap up over the cake to cover and place the cake in the freezer for about 2 hours to set. Reserve the remaining ice cream for another use.

MERINGUE

Combine the egg whites with ⅓ cup (80 g) of the sugar in a medium bowl and, using a handheld mixer, beat on medium-high speed until foamy. On high speed, gradually add the remaining 1 cup (200 g) sugar and continue to beat until the whites are airy, yet stiff. Spoon the meringue into a pastry bag fitted with a plain tip.

Remove the cake from the freezer. Unfold the plastic wrap and place the Roasting & Drip Pan, bottom side down, on top of the bowl. Carefully invert the Roasting & Drip Pan and bowl together, place them on a work surface, lift off the bowl, and peel away the plastic wrap. Pipe the meringue onto the cake, starting at the bottom and working your way up to the top in a turning motion. Make sure the cake is fully covered with meringue. Place the cake in the freezer for at least 4 hours.

TO FINISH

Place the Roasting & Drip Pan topped with the cake on the cooking grid, close the lid of the EGG, and cook for about 12 minutes. The cake will turn a beautiful golden brown. Meanwhile, whisk together the cream and sugar until stiff peaks form. When the cake is ready, remove it from the EGG, and carefully transfer the cake from the Roasting & Drip Pan to a serving plate. Garnish with the whipped cream, the reserved hazelnuts, and the blackberries.

I'VE BEEN COOKING SINCE I WAS SMALL

Reuben Riffel

Perfect Balance in Every Finished Dish

Although luxuries were few and circumstances humble, South African celebrity chef and cooking sensation Reuben Riffel grew up amid a warm family atmosphere where time together was treasured. His grandmother, mother, and aunts would spend hours preparing family feasts, always using the fresh fruits and vegetables grown on his grandfather's small plot of land in the fertile valley of Groendal, Franschhoek, South Africa.

"I've been cooking since I was small," reminisces Reuben. "When I was twelve, one of my duties was starting the wood-burning stove for my mom. When I was fifteen, I started to cook my own food, which caused quite a lot of problems. My mom would shop for food for the week, and I sometimes used things I wasn't supposed to . . . I'd invite friends over and make pasta Bolognese."

Reuben's first job was in the construction trade, and it ended when he became a waiter. It didn't take long for him to migrate behind the scenes into the kitchen, where he was quickly promoted to sous chef. When the chef unexpectedly departed, Reuben was suddenly left to run his first kitchen on his own. Travels across Europe and restaurant success in England exposed Reuben to the complex flavors of European, English, and Irish cuisines. But when friends offered him the opportunity to run his own restaurant—bearing his own name in his own hometown—Reuben returned home. Renowned for his culinary mastery, Reuben describes his cooking style as eclectic and unpretentious. There is an honest simplicity to the food he serves, based on selecting the finest seasonal produce sourced from nearby farms. "I've always been surprised that I can taste something and store it in the back of my mind. Even as a kid, I'd go through the cupboard and look for things that I thought just had to go into a dish to re-create what I'd tasted.

"I try to keep things uncomplicated, bringing out the natural flavors of each ingredient, and I strive for perfect balance in every finished dish," he explains. When cooking on his Big Green Egg, Reuben enjoys not only *braaing*—the Afrikaans word for "grilling"—but also slow roasting, smoking, and baking. "I enjoy the adrenaline of the restaurant scene, but also I like the intimacy of cooking at home, as meals are among the best ways to spend quality time with my family. Making someone a great meal on an EGG is one of the nicest gifts you can give."

www.reubens.co.za

SERVES 4 TO 6	COOKING TIME	GRILL TEMPERATURE	EQUIPMENT
	2½ hours	Set the EGG for indirect cooking with	convEGGtor
	(+ 30 minutes for curing)	the Roasting & Drip Pan under the grid.	Roasting & Drip Pan
		Preheat the EGG to 325°F (165°C).	Stir-Fry and Paella Grill Pan or wok

A quality digital thermometer is a necessity when cooking meat or poultry to monitor the internal temperature safely. Remember, you can't tell if food is safely cooked by looking at it!

PORK BELLY
with poached apricots and curry sauce

Ingredients

PORK BELLY
1 (3⅓-pound/1.5-kg) piece pork belly, fat finely scored
3 tablespoons coarse salt
4 thyme sprigs

POACHED APRICOTS
1 cup (240 ml) water
1 cup (200 g) sugar
2 star anise pods
2 teaspoons ground cinnamon
8 to 12 dried apricots

CURRY SAUCE
1 tablespoon vegetable oil
2 yellow onions, chopped
1 teaspoon chopped garlic
1 teaspoon peeled and chopped fresh ginger
2 tablespoons curry powder
2 tablespoons garam masala (Indian spice blend)
1 tablespoon ground turmeric
1 tablespoon sweet paprika
3 allspice berries
2 bay leaves
½ cup (120 ml) white wine vinegar
1 cup (170 g) whole canned tomatoes
1 cup (240 ml) water
1 cup (240 ml) chicken stock
½ cup (100 g) sugar
1 teaspoon salt
1 teaspoon freshly ground black pepper

Preparation

PORK BELLY
Rub the pork belly evenly with the salt, focusing on the fatty part. Rub in the thyme evenly. Let cure for 30 minutes.

Dust the excess salt off the pork belly and place the pork, fatty side up, on the cooking grid. Close the lid on the EGG and cook for 1 hour and 40 minutes, flipping the pork over halfway through cooking. Transfer the pork belly to a cutting board, tent with aluminum foil, and let rest for 10 minutes before slicing.

POACHED APRICOTS
Combine the water, sugar, star anise, and cinnamon in a small saucepan, place over medium-high heat, and bring to a boil on the stove top, stirring to dissolve the sugar. Turn down the heat to a simmer, add the apricots, and poach for 2 to 3 minutes. Remove from the heat, strain through a fine-mesh sieve, and set aside.

CURRY SAUCE
Increase the temperature in the EGG to 350°F (180°C). Place the oil, onions, garlic, ginger, curry powder, garam masala, turmeric, paprika, allspice, and bay leaves in the Stir-Fry and Paella Grill Pan or wok and place on the cooking grid. Close the lid of the EGG and cook, stirring occasionally, for about 10 minutes, or until the vegetables are soft and the mixture is fragrant. Pour in the vinegar and deglaze the pan, stirring briefly. Close the lid and decrease the temperature to 300°F (150°C).

Add the tomatoes, water, stock, sugar, salt, and pepper, stir well, and close the lid of the EGG. Cook for 20 to 30 minutes, until the sauce thickens to a thick gravy consistency. Remove from the EGG, let cool slightly, transfer to a blender, and process until smooth. Strain through a fine-mesh sieve.

TO FINISH
Serve the pork belly drizzled with the warm curry sauce and with the poached apricots.

my style is
ROUGH
in a
THOUGHTFUL
MANNER

Piet-Hein Vencken
Marathonweg

If you use a picture of the Big Green Egg as the photo on your LinkedIn profile, you've come pretty far as a chef. It says: My oven represents who I am. "Well, no," is Piet-Hein Vencken's reaction, as we talk in Marathonweg, a new restaurant in Amsterdam. "That EGG has a certain image; it's a guy thing. It's just cool. It stands for what I do now."

The young chef is currently working on putting Marathonweg on the map. "Initially, I was going to play an advisory role—design the kitchen, determine the menu. But then I thought to myself, why don't I just do this myself? Prior to Marathonweg, I was working at the restaurant Tijn Akersloot, which was a real assembly line with 700 place settings on a busy day. Here at Marathonweg, we serve about 130 a day. I have a lot more time for detail and to really cook. The idea at Marathonweg is to have an accessible restaurant where everyone can eat for ten to twenty-three euros. And the restaurant is open all day for lunch and dinner." Television chef Alain Caron, Vencken's neighbor, has already tested the menu.

Chef Vencken continues, "We differentiate ourselves with the products we use, for example, by using Brood van Menno [a specialty bakery] and free-range meat. I prepare everything myself, from the mayonnaise to the pies. The owners wanted a grill-style restaurant, which leads us to the Big Green Egg. It is cool that the EGG gives a great look to a business, especially in an open kitchen." The two EGGS do look beautiful in the open kitchen. "It's different than an open grill; you can create a more subtle taste. For example, cooking fish with the skin on in a baking dish, but finishing it on the Big Green Egg. You can barely taste the subtlety, but it's there, in the background. You can never get flavor like that from an ordinary grill."

Piet-Hein Vencken would not describe his cooking style as Nouveau Ruig (as described in Dave De Belder's profile on page 137). "I think my style is more like that of the Hotel de Goudfazant in Amsterdam Noord, which consists of a duct-tape interior, with tables in the garage. My style is rough in a thoughtful manner—simple but good and well thought out. Not simply a steak in a pan, but a beef shoulder and then doing something special with the dish. Or pancetta, or a Black Angus burger with beet chutney, bacon, and tarragon mayonnaise."

Chef Vencken has gone through a lot over the years. First, he had to disregard the contempt of the culinary profession by his classmates. "Back then, cooking was for losers. But I was sure I wanted to go to hotel school." He gained experience working at several restaurants, including Fagel in Naarden, the Amstel Hotel, and the 't Swarte Schaep restaurant in the Leidesplein in Amsterdam. An interlude followed at Nespresso. "I had a 'quarter-life' crisis; I was done with the restaurant business." After eight years in the business world, Vencken missed cooking, so he started the restaurant KEK with his girlfriend on Hoofddorpplein, a well-known square in Amsterdam. It proved successful but was too small to hire more help. "With two small children, it was too much. Working five days a week and cooking thirteen hours a day, I never saw my family. I took a break and then went to Tijn Akersloot, which had a large, well-experienced team and hundreds of customers a day—a real cooking factory.

"So I was ready to start fine-tuning my menu, including slow-roasted pork belly from pigs raised by clergy at a monastery in Limburg with sausage from Brandt & Levie. We are still in the test phase to see how far we can go. A beautiful French dish with corn-fed chicken and a roasted carcass breast. I add a glazed bone with its own drippings and a fresh vegetable. There is diversity in tastes and textures that one would not readily expect in a grill-style restaurant."

Tip: "The first time you use the Big Green Egg, fill the Fire Box all the way to the top with coals. Give it plenty of air, close the lid, open all the air vents, and you'll see how quickly the temperature rises. Adjust the dials and see what happens. The temperature decreases on its own. Be careful of the 'burp' of high heat when you open the EGG at high temperatures. Play around with the dial on top, and soon you'll be a pro."

www.marathonweg.com

COOKING TIME

50 minutes

(+ 8 hours to brine the carcasses, 45 minutes

for the carcasses to rest, 6 to 8 hours to cook the

legs, 2½ to 3 hours to cook the gravy, and 25 to

30 minutes to cook the polenta)

glazed, grilled CHICKEN with gravy, vegetables in GREMOLATA and crusty polenta

Ingredients

CHICKEN

2 free-range chickens

Salt, for making brine

Sea salt, for rubbing

Freshly ground black pepper

GLAZED BONES

5 cups (1 kg) duck fat

2 star anise pods

3 cinnamon sticks

Peel of 1 orange

4 cloves garlic

½ bunch thyme

GRAVY

2¼ pounds (1 kg) chicken wings

1 chicken carcass

1 teaspoon tomato purée

1 pound (450 g) carrots,
peeled and chopped

1 leek, chopped

½ bunch celery,
chopped

1 pound (450 g) yellow onions,
quartered

4 cloves garlic

3½ ounces (100 g) mushrooms,
cleaned and chopped

2 bay leaves

Scant ½ cup (100 ml) red wine

Cold unsalted butter, for thickening

Salt and freshly ground black pepper

CRUSTY POLENTA

1½ cups (375 ml) water

⅔ cup (90 g) cornmeal

3½ tablespoons unsalted butter,
at room temperature

6½ tablespoons (40 g) grated
Parmesan cheese

1 clove garlic, finely chopped

½ teaspoon fine sea salt

Olive oil, for frying

VEGETABLES WITH GREMOLATA

1 pound (450 g) assorted vegetables (such
as green beans, broccoli, carrots, and cherry
tomatoes)

Sugar, for roasting

Salt, for roasting

Olive oil, for roasting and for gremolata

1 cup (50 g) finely chopped fresh flat-leaf parsley

1 teaspoon finely chopped fresh rosemary needles

1 teaspoon finely chopped fresh sage leaves

Grated zest of 1 lemon

1 teaspoon chopped oil-packed anchovy fillets

4 teaspoons minced garlic

Sea salt

Preparation

BRINING CHICKEN

Remove the legs and wings from each chicken and
set them aside. Using a formula of 4 tablespoons
sea salt to 4¼ cups (1 L) water, mix up enough
brine to immerse the whole carcasses with
breasts. Place them in the brine, cover tightly, and
refrigerate for 8 hours. Rub the legs with sea salt
and set aside for 15 minutes. Reserve the wings
for adding to the gravy.

GLAZED BONES

Preheat the oven to 150°F (65°C). Place the legs
in a baking dish and add the duck fat, sea salt, star
anise, cinnamon sticks, orange peel, garlic, and
thyme. Cover the dish with aluminum foil and,
using a fork, prick some holes in the foil. Cook the
legs in the oven for 6 to 8 hours.

COOKING CHICKEN

Remove the carcasses from the brine and pat
dry with a clean kitchen towel. Place the meat
thermometer in the thickest part of a breast and
place the carcasses, meat side up, on the cooking
grid in the EGG. Close the lid of the EGG, wait
for 30 minutes, and then begin checking the
meat thermometer at regular intervals. When the
thermometer registers 150°F (65°C), remove the
carcasses from the EGG and let rest for 45 minutes.

GRAVY

Increase the temperature of the EGG to 425°F
(220°C). Place the chicken wings, including the
reserved wings, and the chicken carcass in the
large baking dish. Add the tomato purée, place
the large baking dish in the EGG, close the lid of
the EGG, and cook for 5 minutes. Transfer the
contents of the baking dish to a large stockpot
and add the carrots, leek, celery, onions, garlic,
mushrooms, bay leaves, wine, and just enough
water to cover. Bring to a boil over medium-high
heat on the stove top, skimming off any foam that
forms on the top. Turn down the heat to low and
simmer for 2 hours. Strain through a fine-mesh
sieve, return to a large clean saucepan, and cook
over medium heat until reduced by two-thirds.

CRUSTY POLENTA

Preheat the oven to 340°F (170°C). Bring the
water to a boil in a small ovenproof saucepan
over high heat. As soon as the water starts to boil,
slowly add the cornmeal while stirring constantly.
Turn down the heat to medium and continue to

cook, stirring constantly, until the cornmeal starts to bind. Cover the polenta with waxed paper, top the pan with a lid, and place in the oven for 20 minutes. Remove the pan from the oven, add the butter, cheese, garlic, and salt, and stir well. Pour the polenta into a small shallow baking dish, let cool, cover, and refrigerate. Just before ready to serve, unmold the polenta and cut into cubes or slices.

VEGETABLES WITH GREMOLATA
Preheat the EGG to 425°F (220°C). If using the cherry tomatoes, place them in the small baking dish with some sugar, salt, and olive oil and place the baking dish in the EGG. Close the lid of the EGG and cook the tomatoes until their skins

start to wrinkle and they begin to collapse. Set aside. Trim and cut the remaining vegetables as needed. Bring a large saucepan filled with water to a boil on the stove top and blanch each vegetable until tender-crisp. Combine the tomatoes and blanched vegetables in a bowl.

To make the gremolata, in a small bowl, combine the parsley, rosemary, sage, lemon zest, anchovies, and garlic and stir to mix. Add oil to the herb mixture until it is somewhat fluid. Season the gremolata with sea salt, then add to the vegetables and mix gently.

TO FINISH
Remove the legs from the duck fat and place them in a nonstick frying pan. Place the pan over medium heat on the stove top and cook until

the skin become crispy, adding some duck fat if needed to prevent sticking.

Cut each chicken carcass lengthwise to create 4 half breasts total. Place the breasts on the grid in the EGG, close the lid of the EGG, and cook the breasts for just a little longer. Be careful not to overcook. Cut the breast meat off the carcasses. Heat a little oil in a frying pan over medium heat on the stove top and fry the polenta until golden on all sides. Pour the reduced stock for the gravy into a blender and process with enough cold butter to thicken. Season with salt and pepper. Let your inner chef out and arrange the plates using the photograph for guidance or mere inspiration!

I don't do RECIPES

Esther Gerlsma
Tandjong Priok Arum

If the Big Green Egg has an honorable position anywhere, it is surely at Tandjong Priok. The Indonesian restaurant on a farm in Friesland has a colonial interior, ship clocks hanging on the walls, wayang puppets (Indonesian shadow puppets) on display, and then, between the tables, the moss-colored grill. The Big Green Egg is not found in the kitchen or outside on the lawn, but inside, among the guests, where a pig, prepared Balinese style (*babi guling*), has been roasting for eleven hours. Laughing, chef Esther Gerlsma says the butcher has given her an exceptionally large pig, and she was barely able to get it into the EGG. Normally, she uses the EGG for small chickens.

Is this a Balinese recipe from a chef who hails from Sumatra? "I am not choosy," says Esther affably. She wants to prepare dishes from all corners of the Indonesian archipelago and share them at her restaurant in Arum, Friesland. She attempts to make every dish as authentic as possible, explaining, "I will not make concessions when it comes to taste. Everything that comes to the table has gone through my hands." She is prepared to go far in that regard. If certain spices aren't available, the importer is called. And if the importer doesn't have what she's looking for, she makes a call to the exporter in Jakarta. Esther needed *ruku-ruku*, an Indonesian variety of basil that her exporter had never heard of, so she called her family in southern Sumatra, who found a local supplier. "A week later a bag arrived with thirty-three pounds of *ruku-ruku*," she said, triumphantly. "Now I have a good supply in the freezer."

She also met her husband, Sicco Gerlsma, in southern Sumatra, in the province of Lampung, and ten years ago they decided to settle in Arum. Esther grew up living with an aunt and uncle who grew vegetables and rice, and she quickly learned about different types of foods, "literally from A to Z." She discovered the sweet side of Indonesian cooking, the Javanese side, from her parents, and she also lived on Bali for six months. She does not use written recipes, she prepares everything by hand, and she regularly flies back to Indonesia to delve further into the local cuisine. Her favorite regional cuisine is found in Padang, the culinary capital of western Sumatra. "The manner of cooking is very different there," Esther explains. "The locals like to say that, 'when you eat, you eat with your nose, ears, and tongue.' Padang cooking is a total flavor explosion, famous throughout Indonesia."

Initially, the residents in Friesland thought a new Chinese Indonesian restaurant had opened in their corner of the world. Esther made quick work of that misconception. There was not going to be *babi panggang* (Indonesian slang for Chinese pork dishes) at her restaurant. "Everything has to be authentic—as real as you can find in Indonesia. We have been in business for eight years now and are building a loyal customer base, which is why we have a different menu every week. People can choose from twenty different types of satay followed by various tasting options. For those who want fresh sambal [hot chili sauce], we prepare the sauce at the table." Esther and Sicco Gerlsma learned about the Big Green Egg through social media. They enjoyed the EGG presentation given by ambassador Leonard Elenbaas of Pure Passie, who inspired them to buy one. "The EGG gives me even more ways to cook, such as cooking this pig very slowly, maybe twenty hours, if necessary," says Esther. "If I want it crispier, I just open the air vents. In Bali, they thread a whole pig on a spear and turn it over an open fire. That won't work inside here."

There are plenty of plans for the future, including opening a second restaurant in Leeuwarden, where Esther and Sicco hope to serve lunch. Indonesian food quite literally and figuratively fits with the Slow Food movement. "Beef is cooked in coconut milk for a long period of time, and then it can be preserved naturally for a month or two. We do not have to throw anything away here. And, of course, we work with the best suppliers. In the future, I want to experiment with more locally produced goods. I would like to smoke local geese and fish or maybe prepare them in another Indonesian manner. We are very close to the Waddenzee [intertidal zone on the North Sea] here, so there is still plenty for me to discover."

www.tandjongpriok.nl

SERVES 50 TO 60

COOKING TIME

12 hours

(+ 45 minutes to cook

the cassava leaves)

GRILL TEMPERATURE

Set the EGG for indirect cooking.

Preheat the EGG to 200°F (100°C).

EQUIPMENT

convEGGtor

Small bamboo skewers, soaked

in water, or metal skewers

Meat thermometer

babi guling PIG filled with SPICES and cassava

The cassava in the belly of the pig adds delicious flavor to the meat, and the meat, in turn, gives flavor to the cassava. This dish is perfect for serving a large group. For a traditional feast, serve with white rice, a Balinese sambal (hot chili sauce), and, if you can find it, jackfruit.

Ingredients

4½ pounds (2 kg) frozen chopped cassava leaves

5½ ounces (150 g) fresh turmeric root

9 ounces (250 g) shallots

1 cup (150 g) garlic cloves

5½ ounces (150 g) candlenuts

⅓ cup (30 g) coriander seeds

3 tablespoons white peppercorns

3 tablespoons black peppercorns

2 tablespoons ground nutmeg

2 teaspoons ground cumin

1 cup (100 g) peeled and sliced fresh ginger

1 cup (100 g) peeled and sliced fresh Laos ginger, galangal, or Thai ginger

1 cup (100 g) peeled and sliced fresh kentjoer (aromatic ginger)

1 teaspoon whole cloves

1½ tablespoons shrimp paste

1½ tablespoons plus 1 teaspoon salt

1 (28½ to 37½-pound/13 to 17-kg) suckling pig

3 ounces (80 g) small fresh red chiles, sliced into rings

7 bay leaves

5 lemon leaves (3½ ounces/100 g)

Preparation

In a large saucepan, combine the cassava leaves with water to cover, bring to a boil over high heat, and boil for about 45 minutes, or until tender. Drain and set aside. Peel the turmeric or not as you like. Place a little more than three-fourths of it in a blender and set the remainder aside. Add the shallots, garlic, candlenuts, coriander seeds, white and black peppercorns, nutmeg, cumin, all three gingers, the cloves, the shrimp paste, and 1½ tablespoons of the salt to the blender and process until a paste forms. (Or, use a mortar and pestle to grind to a paste.)

Clean the pig inside and out. Rub the inside of the pig with 4 tablespoons of the spice mixture. Grate the reserved turmeric and rub it and the remaining 1 teaspoon salt on the outside of the pig. Combine the chiles, bay leaves, lemon leaves, the remaining spice paste, and the cooked cassava in a large bowl and mix well. Fill the pig's belly with the cassava-spice mixture and use the skewers to secure the belly closed. Place the meat thermometer in the pig away from bone.

A 37½-pound (17 kg) suckling pig is a good weight for the Big Green Egg, even the XLarge EGG. Place the pig on the cooking grid, close the lid of the EGG, and cook for 12 hours, keeping the temperature at about 200°F (100°C) throughout the cooking. Use the meat thermometer to ensure the desired internal temperature of 155°F (70°C) is reached. Once the pig is done, let it rest for 30 minutes.

TO FINISH

Remove the skin from the pig and portion the meat. Serve each portion with some of the cassava from the belly.

FIRE GIVES
one a primal feeling, and what is simpler than starting a FIRE

Julius Jaspers
Julius Bar & Grill

"Truth be told, I saw that crazy-looking green thing, a little one, at chef Marco Westmaas's restaurant, Elzenduin Beach. Then I saw it at Jonnie Boer's restaurant, De Librije. I waited another three years, and that's when the love began. I immediately bought a large one. The first six months I cursed it. I became totally crazy and desperate! It didn't do what I wanted it to do; it didn't go well. I really had to get used to a barbecue with the lid closed. I was at the point of getting rid of it. And then it all came together. The Big Green Egg is all about heat control. Two things: air vent on the bottom and air vent on the lid. If you know how to fine-tune it, you are king."

A television chef (321 episodes on *Topchef* with stern-looking companion Robert Kranenborgh), *SMART* cookbook writer, and an extraordinary ego, Julius Jaspers is in principal a man of excess: in his activities, his affections, and his jam-packed agenda. The restaurant, Julius Bar & Grill on Ceintuurbaan in Amsterdam, was preparing to open during this interview, and Jaspers was busy picking out china and cutlery. He wants what he wants and gets it. "A plate is a plate and not just stone tile," he says. But when it comes to talking about his big love, the Big Green Egg, Julius frees up time.

He also freed up time when he entered a cooking championship with the Big Green Egg. He assembled a barbecue team, De Zwarte Hand, with team members Jeroen Hazebroek from the Big Green Egg, pastry chef Mathijs Fontein, Michiel Deenik, and Arjan Wennekes from Visaandeschelde restaurant. They all traveled to Morocco for the world championship cook-off. "We came in ninth," Julius says, "but our chicken thighs were certainly winners for us, at least in a morale sense." Jaspers now organizes the Amsterdam BBQ Challenge, where amateurs challenge the professionals. "There is a lot of good talent out there. I am not pessimistic."

Jaspers has just published the *SMART BBQ* cookbook, with which he hopes to convince more people about his fiery passion: there is nothing more beautiful than grilling. "Grilling seldom happens in the Netherlands, and it is very bad. Most men who barbecue think they do it really well because most women encourage their husbands to cook. Even if the meal is charred and overcooked, it is still eaten. I am on a mission to change all that. The notion that barbecue is only enjoyed in the summer is the first misconception that needs to be addressed. Winter is a great time to barbecue!" It's good that Jaspers, with his book and barbecue restaurant (and a barbecue sauce and a ketchup for sale), readily admits he has a commercial interest in promoting the glory of the barbecue. "I don't hold it against people if they see me as a barbecue guru. With a grill, you can make the most beautiful things, which is why I want a big open fire pit in the middle of my restaurant, and right next to it, two Big Green Eggs. It's going to be a large restaurant with seating for about 130 people and with fast service, which works well with an open fire. Otherwise, I would put in fifteen Big Green Eggs, but that's not doable. One Big Green Egg I will use for slow cooking meat. Just yesterday I tried a nice piece of rib-eye from the new menu. The second EGG, which will be constantly set at 350°F [180°C], works as an oven for baking chocolate cakes or *tarte Tatin* or for cooking bowls of garnishes."

But the restaurant is not only about grilling meat. Fish and produce also have an important place on the menu. "Let's take a piece of tuna as an example. The EGG gives the fish more flavor. Just sear it quickly on the outside so it doesn't lose much moisture." Jaspers really likes the flavor that grilling gives fish. "A smoky taste also works well. Experimenting with wood chips, using fresh thyme on the coals, anything is possible." In the end, the real art comes from doing very little. All you need is some fresh fennel, a good-quality olive oil, and a nice balsamic—done.

At one time Julius and a friend owned a restaurant, and after working very hard for a few years, they closed it. After the endless hours and making very little money, he was done. "I am never doing this again," he shouted at the time. And now he's at it again? "It will be different," he swears. "This time I have the support of the entire back office of Bert van der Lede's team. I don't have to build from the ground up. They take care of all the hassle of the renovation, and I can concentrate on the menu and those kinds of things." He won't work twelve-hour shifts anymore or be the chef. Instead, he'll be the restaurateur (think of Joop Braakhekke at Le Garage)—a host who makes sure everything is running well and springs into action to avoid any mishaps.

If there is any time to rest, Julius jumps in the car with his wife and kids, puts the small EGG in the trunk, and they go skiing. "I drag it up four flights of stairs to the apartment. Well, yes, the kids. They get a wonderful meal in return."

www.smartday.nl

SERVES 6	COOKING TIME	GRILL TEMPERATURE	EQUIPMENT
	20 minutes	Set the EGG for direct cooking.	Baking dish
		Preheat the EGG to 375°F (190°C).	Instant-read thermometer

Fish on the Big Green Egg? Of course, anything is possible! The best part is that very little is needed to prepare great-tasting food. Serve the fish whole with a homemade rémoulade sauce seasoned with mixed herbs, such as parsley, chives, and tarragon.

Dorade ENCRUSTED IN SALT

Ingredients

1 (4-pound/1.8-kg) whole dorade (gilt-head bream) or mahimahi, cleaned
1 fennel bulb, cut into chunks
4½ pounds (2 kg) coarse sea salt

Preparation

Pat the fish dry and fill the cavity with the fennel chunks. Place a thick layer of salt in the bottom of the baking dish and place the fish on top. In a large bowl, combine the remaining salt with water in a ratio of 2 cups (420 g) salt to 1 cup (240 ml) water to create a mixture with the consistency of wet sand. Make sure it is not too sticky. Pat the salt mixture evenly over the fish, covering it completely. Place the baking dish on the cooking grid and close the lid of the EGG. After 20 minutes, use the instant-read thermometer to check the temperature of the fish. It should register 140°F (60°C).

TO FINISH
Remove the baking dish from the EGG and let the fish rest for a couple of minutes, then carefully break the salt crust away from the fish. Remove as much salt from the fish as possible before serving.

if you don't MOVE FORWARD, you will come to A STANDSTILL

Peter Goossens

Hof van Cleve

Good wine does not require laurels. Quality sells itself. Well, of course, three Michelin Guide stars do not hurt, either. And if your establishment also rises from a rating of forty-six to twenty-five in *Restaurant Magazine*, you must be doing something right. But for Peter Goossens, the highest-ranked international chef in Belgium, it's never good enough. "If you don't move forward, you will come to a standstill," he reports from the town of Kruishoutem, where he opened his restaurant, Hof van Cleve, more than two decades ago. "I am striving to make it to the top ten next year."

In his farmhouse in the Flemish region below Ghent, he uses fresh, high-quality products daily. His most recent cookbook, *Passie Voor Product* (Passion for Product), highlights the importance of relying on nearby sources. "We process the most beautiful regional products that are supplied by local gardeners, farmers, growers, fishermen, hunters, and cheese makers. Those ingredients determine the DNA of my kitchen. I think it's a beautiful evolution in gastronomy when products move to the forefront. For example, in the Flemish kitchen, produce has always been prominent and continues to play a key role."

Peter Goossens acts on his word and always has a special menu that includes "field, garden, and forest" items. "It is fun to bring something besides a salad with carrots to the table, like Potato Nicola, which has sage, alliums, and celery root, or a dish made with shallots, red beets, chickpeas, and black truffles. Demand for this type of dining came not only from vegetarians, but also from business people who wanted to try something new and eat lighter fare."

About eight years ago, Goossens discovered the Big Green Egg. "I saw the quality was very good and dishes that came out were consistent. The EGG I bought then is still standing in my kitchen today. It is unbreakable and very tough. We use it for grilling and barbecuing. It offers an extra cooking technique that creates a slightly roasted and smoky flavor that adds another dimension to the taste palate. And you can incorporate that smoky flavor in a very precise manner, without dominating the taste."

Goossens enthusiastically adds, "All kinds of meats work well on the grill, not just steak or a beef shoulder. Think about dove or wild duck grilled very lightly. Combine the dove with porcini mushrooms and parsley root, which provide a pleasing balance. Fish is also perfect for the Big Green Egg, but you have to watch it closely or it will break apart. When it comes to cooking vegetables on the EGG, I think celery root turns out particularly well. Cook it lightly on the stove top first and then grill it on the EGG. The beauty of the EGG is that with the lid on, you can keep everything under control—a smoky taste combined with a crispy texture."

www.hofvancleve.com

GRILL TEMPERATURE

Set the EGG for direct cooking. Preheat the EGG to 355°F (180°C).

ANJOU DOVE
with smoke-flavored au jus, glazed parsley root, and porcini mushrooms

This is a classic of the French kitchen. Like the duck, the dove is a highly regarded bird in gastronomy. Here, it is paired with two iconic fall flavors, parsley root and mushrooms.

Ingredients

DOVES

4 (1-pound/450-g) Anjou doves, cleaned
Coarse salt and freshly ground black pepper
1½ cups (300 g) goose or duck fat
Unsalted butter, for cooking

AU JUS

⅓ cup (80 g) unsalted butter, plus 1 chunk cold butter
2 shallots, finely chopped
½ clove garlic
Scant ½ cup (100 ml) red wine
1 bay leaf
⅔ cup (150 ml) brown stock or good-quality beef stock
Freshly ground black pepper

PORCINI MUSHROOMS

14 ounces (400 g) small porcini mushrooms, cleaned
3 tablespoons unsalted butter, plus more for seasoning
Salt and freshly ground black pepper

PARSLEY ROOT

1 (14-ounce/400-g) parsley root
2½ tablespoons unsalted butter
1 teaspoon ground mace
Salt and freshly ground black pepper
1 cup (240 ml) chicken stock
2 tablespoons sugar

Small watercress leaves, for garnish

Preparation

DOVES

Remove the whole legs with the oysters intact from the doves. Place the legs and the dove carcasses with breasts in a shallow bowl, sprinkle well with salt and pepper, and let sit for 15 minutes. Preheat the oven to 200°F (100°C). Rinse all the dove pieces thoroughly and pat dry. Place the pieces in the goose fat in a baking pan and cook in the oven for 1 hour. Remove the pieces from the goose fat. Transfer the fat to a heatproof container, let cool, cover, and refrigerate for another use. Wrap the legs in plastic wrap and set aside (the plastic wrap keeps the shape of the legs nicely).

Season the dove carcasses with breasts inside and out with salt and pepper. Place a few tablespoons of butter in the Dutch Oven or ovenproof saucepan, place the Dutch Oven in the EGG, close the lid, and heat just until the butter foams. Place the carcasses with breasts in the Dutch Oven, close the lid of the EGG, and cook, turning once, for 4 minutes on each side. Remove the Dutch Oven from the EGG, then remove the dove pieces and let rest for a few minutes.

Bone the breasts from the carcasses and cover the breast fillets with aluminum foil to keep warm. Place the carcasses on the cooking grid in the EGG, close the lid, and cook for about 10 more minutes. Set the carcasses aside to use for making the smoke-flavored au jus.

Unwrap the reserved dove legs, place them in the Dutch Oven, and season with salt and pepper. Transfer to the EGG, close the lid, and heat the legs just until warm. Remove the Dutch Oven from the EGG, then remove the legs and cover with aluminum foil to keep warm.

AU JUS

Transfer the Dutch Oven to the stove top, add the ⅓ cup (80 g) butter, and melt over medium heat. Add the shallots and garlic and cook gently for a few minutes, or until tender. Add the reserved carcasses and sauté for a few minutes. Pour in the wine and deglaze the pan, stirring to dislodge any browned bits. Add the bay leaf and let the liquid boil down. Add the stock and heat until the liquid is reduced by half. Remove from the heat and strain through a fine-mesh sieve into a saucepan. Reheat over medium-low heat and then whisk in the cold butter to finish. Season with pepper and keep warm.

PORCINI MUSHROOMS

Thinly slice the mushrooms vertically. Heat the butter in a medium frying pan over medium heat on the stove top. Add the mushrooms and sauté briefly, just until lightly browned. Season with salt and pepper and then stir in more butter if needed for flavor. (Optional: Remove 1 uncooked mushroom from the batch; finely dice it; and marinate it in olive oil, salt, and pepper to use for garnish.)

PARSLEY ROOT

Peel the parsley root and slice into long strips. Melt about half of the butter in a medium saucepan over medium heat on the stove top. Add the parsley root and mace and sauté for several minutes, or until just tender. Season well with salt and pepper, then add the stock, sugar, and the remaining butter and bring to a boil. Boil the mixture until the pan is dry and the butter and sugar have formed a light coating on the parsley root strips. (Optional: Purée a few parsley root slices until smooth, add a splash of heavy cream, and use for garnish.)

TO FINISH

Arrange the parsley root and mushrooms on each plate. Garnish with the parsley root cream and minced raw mushroom, if using. Place the dove fillet alongside the parsley root and mushrooms and finish with the reserved legs and a few leaves of watercress. Serve the warm au jus on the side.

I LEARNED TO COOK TO SURVIVE

Raghavan Iyer
A Cuisine of Spices

More than thirty years ago, Mumbai-native Raghavan Iyer left India to fulfill his dream of enrolling in a college program in hotel and restaurant management. "I arrived in the United States with a degree in chemistry but was pretty clueless about cooking. I learned to cook to survive," says the self-taught chef. "My skill and creativity evolved over time, and my meals became much more elaborate, because I was learning techniques that I could apply to the flavors of my childhood. I love the Indian curries, which are traditional sauce-based dishes, but I don't define myself with one particular style of cooking. . . . I'm a spice and flavor guy."

After graduating from Michigan State, Iyer worked in a restaurant, learning about the commercial end of cooking. "I loved the energy of the restaurant, but I felt that being in the operations end of the kitchen stymied my creativity. I always wanted to teach, so I started teaching about cooking. The teaching led to writing, and the writing, of course, led to the books. My growing curiosity about Indian regional cuisines led to a new career, and life took on a whole new meaning.

"Centuries ago, the world came to India because of its native spices— mustard, fennel, black peppercorns, cumin—and these flavors were spread around the world by spice traders traveling the Silk Road, so that now these spices season the cuisines of many different cultures. These same traders also introduced their own cooking techniques to India, and we embraced those and made them part of our own. When you think of Indian food, you think of spices. You think of the world of flavors.

"The first time I cooked with a Big Green Egg, I made naan on the baking stone. The EGG reminds me so much of an Indian tandoor oven, with its ability to consistently hold high temperatures. Now one of my favorites is naan pizza. . . . I partially bake the bread before I throw on all the ingredients . . . the crust and flavors are unbelievable!

"On my XLarge Big Green Egg, I make a roasted lamb rubbed with cardamom, garlic, and red chile. That lamb dish taught me the real beauty of the even heat you get when cooking on the EGG. Then there is delicious traditional chicken tandoori . . . this is such a beautiful way of roasting a bird at a high temperature to keep it more succulent. And in the summer, I roast vegetables from my garden in the EGG in my yard. Cooking outdoors on the EGG is like an extension of your kitchen. I see it as a complete system that opens your eyes to cooking techniques that you never thought you could try outside."

www.raghavaniyer.com

SERVES 4

COOKING TIME
10 minutes
(+ up to overnight to marinate)

GRILL TEMPERATURE
Set the EGG for direct cooking.
Preheat the EGG to 400°F (200°C).

EQUIPMENT
Stir-Fry and Paella Grill Pan or wok

The perfect balance of simple spices yields creamy results for sweet scallops—a combination that is nothing short of perfection. Serve the scallops with steamed white rice (preferably basmati) for a quick and delicious meal.

CARDAMOM
fennel scallops

Ingredients

SPICE BLEND
1 teaspoon fennel seeds
½ teaspoon black or yellow mustard seeds
¼ teaspoon cardamom seeds

SCALLOPS
12 large sea scallops
4 cloves garlic, finely chopped
2 dried hot red chiles (such as árbol), coarsely chopped with seeds
1 teaspoon kosher salt or coarse sea salt
2 tablespoons canola oil
½ cup (120 ml) unsweetened coconut milk

1 tablespoon finely chopped fresh cilantro leaves and tender stems, for garnish

Preparation

SPICE BLEND
Place the fennel seeds, mustard seeds, and cardamom seeds in a spice grinder (or a clean coffee grinder) and grind until the consistency of finely ground black pepper. (Be sure to take a good sniff as you open the lid and be prepared for a burst of flavor!) Transfer the spice blend to a medium bowl.

SCALLOPS
Add the scallops, garlic, chiles, and salt to the spice blend and turn the scallops to coat evenly with the seasonings. Cover and refrigerate the scallops until you are ready to cook them. Because there is nothing acidic in the seasoning mix, the scallops can be left to marinate overnight.

When you are ready to cook the scallops, place the oil in the Stir-Fry and Paella Grill Pan or wok, place on the cooking grid, close the lid of the EGG, and heat for 1 to 2 minutes, until the oil shimmers. Add the scallops to the pan, arranging them in a single layer. Close the lid of the EGG and sear the scallops for 2 minutes on each side, or until light reddish brown.

Pour the coconut milk into the pan. It will immediately start to bubble. Scrape the bottom of the pan to release all the browned bits. Close the lid of the EGG and let the scallops simmer, without stirring, for about 2 minutes, or until just firm to the touch. Transfer the scallops to a serving platter.

Let the sauce continue to simmer, stirring occasionally, until thickened, about 2 minutes.

TO FINISH
Pour the pan sauce over the scallops and sprinkle with the cilantro.

when I think of barbecue, I THINK OF lukewarm beer AND BURNED PORK CHOPS: an insult to the BGE

Hidde de Brabander
Dreams of Magnolia

Hidde de Brabander is a man on a mission. The Dutch pastry chef is up at five thirty every morning in his atelier, Dreams of Magnolia, in the industrial area of The Hague. He sizes up his day, answers e-mail, and thinks about ideas for new recipes. His taste palate is fresh in the morning. "When it is nice and quiet, I can get twenty-five new ideas for nougat in a very short time."

He talks about one of his success stories, Single Malt Nougat. It is a hearty nougat bar with a combination of Isle of Islay single malt whisky and Dalmore King Alexander III whisky. It also has almonds that are smoked on the Big Green Egg with wood chips soaked in sixty-year-old whisky barrels from Scotland. "This makes a perfect combination with oysters soaked in brine, and, of course, a whisky." De Brabander will cook fifty-five pounds of almonds at a time, which gives him an ample supply for his website sales. He also sells to the Dutch restaurant and catering business. He does not own a brick-and-mortar store. He thinks it is too dull to make the same custards, cakes, and pastries every day and then wait to see if customers feel like ordering them again.

Hidde started baking in western Holland as a fifteen-year-old, because even as a young boy he knew that he wanted to bake. Actually, he wanted to become a sculptor. In the end, he saw becoming a pastry chef as an art form, as well. Now he combines the two hobbies: eating sweets and creating art.

But learning the art of preparing puddings and pastries was not enough for a young, ambitious, studious pastry chef. A long training process followed at the chic Huize van Wely in Noordwijk, famous for its pastries and chocolates, and at Patisserie de Rouw in Vught. "I noticed that sector of cooking had very little, if any, innovation. The whole year through it was the same old strawberry tart and then in August came the *speculaas* [gingerbread]. I knew I wanted to be in the hospitality industry because there were more possibilities." And so he became a pastry chef at the then newly opened Duin en Kruidberg, a large hotel in northern Holland. "I had four people working under me and had to make desserts on the premises. It wasn't easy; in fact, it was quite difficult. But I didn't want to throw in the towel, so instead I sprinted forward and held my head above water. The hotel quickly made it to the top one hundred best restaurants in Holland, and I had the good fortune to be a part of that."

Again, driven by his ambitions ("I was twenty-four and too young for a regular routine"), Hidde relocated to Parkheuvel to work under Cees Helder. A year later, he was working at De Librije with Jonnie Boers. "Helder was the amiable gentleman, and Jonnie would come to work in his gym shoes, but both have reached extraordinary culinary heights."

Ultimately, it came down to Hidde wanting to start his own business. "I didn't just want to turn out products. I wanted to develop things on my own, give lessons, do some catering, have total freedom. That's why it's so nice that the hospitality industry embraces my products. They want something special, preferably custom-made, like the Single Malt Nougat."

Hidde uses his enormous Big Green Egg regularly in his line of work, and it has a prominent place in the middle of his kitchen. "I first saw it at De Librije, but I didn't use it until later. Look, an oven is an oven, and a knife is a knife. But a barbecue can only be the Big Green Egg." It is a cool machine with its own tastes. He likens it to "having quality window shades; they enhance and don't take anything away. When I think of traditional barbecue, I think of lukewarm beer and burned pork chops: an insult to the Big Green Egg."

Hidde is crazy about the ceramic EGG and the subtle smoky flavor it imparts. "The taste really gets in there. The fewer wood chips you use, the nicer the taste. With an open barbecue a lot of the taste and aroma is just blown away, but not with the EGG." The preparation of meat and fish is fairly obvious, but "the combination of sweet and smoky is an absolute winner. I think it's sad when we stuff ourselves at family barbecues with bread and salads and then eat the long-awaited meat, leaving no room for dessert."

Certain desserts pick up an extra dimension from the EGG. De Brabander likes to smoke chocolate cake with cherry wood chips. Heating the EGG to 155°F (70°C) "is how you reach depth with flavors. Raspberries, roasted peppers, everything is possible. You can compare it to drinking coffee: first you drink it with some milk and sugar and then you switch over to espresso."

For those who can't wait to taste Hidde's creations, he is planning to build a tasting room. Not a tearoom, not a bakery, but like it's done in Barcelona, where you can go to a spot and eat "*à la minute,*" Hidde delights.

Tip: "If you buy a Big Green Egg, allow yourself time to experiment. Don't see it as a rushed job, but discover the fun. We live in a 'plug and play' world, where everything is ready to use, but the EGG is not in that category. It is very easy to use, but you must learn how to go about it. It is a very basic tool: you are working with live fire and you have everything in your hands. With patisserie cooking, it's all about precise temperatures, so learn how to master the fire."

www.dreamsofmagnolia.nl

COOKING TIME

10 minutes

(+ 25 minutes to cool the cake, 10 minutes
to bake the crumble, and 2½ hours to cool
and chill the ice cream base)

GRILL TEMPERATURE

Set the EGG for indirect cooking.
Preheat the EGG to 380°F (195°C).

EQUIPMENT

convEGGtor

15½ by 10½ by 1-inch (39 by 26.5 by 2.5-cm)

jelly roll pan

Grill Gripper

Perforated Cooking Grid (rectangular or round)

MANGO
SMOKED ON LAPSANG SOUCHONG TEA LEAVES
with milk chocolate cake and maple ice cream

Certain desserts pick up an extra dimension from the Big Green Egg. The combination of sweet and smoky is an absolute winner.

Ingredients

CAKE

10½ ounces (300 g) milk chocolate, chopped

1⅓ cups (300 g) unsalted butter

4 eggs

5 egg yolks

⅔ cup (120 g) sugar

1 cup (125 g) all-purpose flour

MAPLE ICE CREAM

1½ cups (360 ml) heavy cream

1½ cups (360 ml) whole milk

1 cup (200 g) sugar

½ vanilla bean, split lengthwise

3 tablespoons maple syrup

CRUMBLE

1 cup plus 1½ tablespoons (250 g) unsalted
butter, cut into cubes

½ cup (100 g) sugar

2 eggs

½ cup (100 g) broyage (1 part each sugar and
almond flour)

3⅔ cups (450 g) all-purpose flour

SMOKED MANGO

Handful of Lapsang souchong tea leaves

2 mangoes, peeled, pitted, and cut into large
slices 1½ inches (4 cm) thick

Good-quality store-bought caramel sauce,
for garnish

Preparation

CAKE

Butter the 15½ by 10½ by 1-inch (39 by 26.5 by 2.5-cm) jelly roll pan, then line with parchment paper. Combine the chocolate and butter in the top of a double boiler over simmering water and heat, stirring occasionally, until smooth. Pour into a medium bowl. In a separate bowl, beat together the eggs, egg yolks, and sugar until the sugar dissolves and the mixture lightens in color. Add the flour to the chocolate mixture and mix together with a rubber spatula. Using the spatula, fold the chocolate-flour mixture into the egg mixture, mixing well. Pour the batter into the prepared pan. Place the pan on the cooking grid in the EGG, close the lid of the EGG, and cook for 5 minutes. Let cool on a wire rack for 25 minutes, then invert onto a cutting board and peel off the parchment. Cut into 4 rectangles and 24 diferent-size circles and set aside.

MAPLE ICE CREAM

Combine the cream, milk, and sugar in a medium saucepan over medium heat on the stove top, stirring until the sugar dissolves. Continue to cook until small bubbles form around the edges of the pan, then remove from the heat. Using tip of a knife, scrape the seeds from the vanilla bean into the cream mixture and then add the pod. Stir in the maple syrup, let stand for 30 minutes, and then cover and chill for at least 2 hours. Remove and discard the vanilla pod, transfer the mixture to an ice cream maker, and freeze according to the manufacturer's directions. Transfer the ice cream to an airtight container and place in the freezer until serving.

CRUMBLE

Preheat the oven to 350°F (180°C). Combine the butter and sugar in a food processor and pulse until crumbly. Add the eggs, one at a time, processing after each addition until combined. Add the broyage and flour and pulse until combined. On a lightly floured work surface, knead the dough until smooth, then roll it out into a rectangle (it does not need to be perfect) and transfer to a baking sheet. Bake for about 10 minutes , or until golden and set. Let cool and then crumble.

MANGO

Using the Grill Gripper, remove the grid from the EGG and then carefully remove the convEGGtor. Lower the temperature of the EGG to 195°F (90°C). Sprinkle the tea leaves on the hot coals, place the cooking grid in the EGG, and top with the Perforated Cooking Grid. Place the mangoes on the Perforated Cooking Grid, close the lid of the EGG, and smoke the mangoes for about 5 minutes. Transfer the mangoes to a cutting board. Using small round cookie cutters of various sizes or a small pairing knife, cut out 16 different-size pieces of mango.

TO FINISH

Randomly arrange 1 rectangle and 6 circles of cake on each serving piece. Place 4 pieces of smoked mango around the cake and top the cake and mango with a light sprinkling of the crumble. Place a small scoop of ice cream on the side and finish with several drops of caramel sauce.

mango **BGE**

EQUIPMENT	GRILL TEMPERATURE	COOKING TIME	SERVES 8
convEGGtor	Set the EGG for indirect cooking.	55 minutes	
Pizza & Baking Stone	Preheat the EGG to 340°F (170°C).	(+ 10 minutes to cook the meringue)	

YUZU CRÈME
with toasted meringue and
BRETON CAKE

Serve this dessert on a well-worn pizza stone.

Ingredients

BRETON CAKE

2⅔ tablespoons egg yolks (2 to 3 egg yolks)

⅓ cup (80 g) sugar

⅓ cup (80 g) unsalted butter, at room temperature, cut into chunks

1 cup (120 g) all-purpose flour

¾ teaspoon baking powder

¼ teaspoon salt

CRÈME

8 yuzu

⅔ cup (120 g) sugar

4 teaspoons cornstarch

⅔ cup (160 ml) heavy cream

⅓ cup (100 g) eggs (about 2 eggs)

¼ cup (60 g) egg yolks (about 3 egg yolks)

Scant ½ cup (100 ml) yuzu syrup

MERINGUE

Scant ½ cup (100 ml) water

2 cups (400 g) sugar

¾ cup (200 g) egg whites (about 7 egg whites)

Edible gold leaf, for garnish

Preparation

BRETON CAKE

Line the bottom of an 8-inch (20-cm) round cake pan with parchment paper and butter the parchment. In a medium bowl, beat together the egg yolks and sugar until the sugar dissolves and the mixture lightens in color. Add the butter and beat until smooth. Sift together the flour, baking powder, and salt into a small bowl. Add the flour mixture to the egg mixture and beat until smooth. Pour the batter into the prepared pan. Place the pan on the cooking grid in the EGG, close the lid of the EGG, and cook for about 25 minutes, or until set. Let cool on a wire rack, then turn the cake out the pan, peel off the parchment, and crumble the cake. Set the crumbs aside.

CRÈME

Cut a thin slice off the top of each yuzu and scoop out the pulp with a small spoon. Set aside. Lower the temperature of the EGG to 200°F (100°C), place the Pizza & Baking Stone on the grid, and close the lid to preheat. In a medium bowl, stir together the sugar and cornstarch. Add the cream, eggs, egg yolks, and yuzu syrup and mix well. Pour into the hollowed-out yuzu and sprinkle with the reserved cake crumbs. Place the yuzu on the Pizza & Baking Stone in the EGG, close the lid of the EGG, and cook for about 30 minutes.

MERINGUE

Combine the water and 1½ cups (300 g) of the sugar in a medium saucepan over high heat and bring to a boil, stirring to dissolve the sugar. Once the mixture is at a boil, stop stirring and heat until the sugar syrup registers 240°F (115°C) on a candy thermometer. Meanwhile, in a medium bowl, combine the egg whites and the remaining ½ cup (100 g) sugar and, using a handheld mixer, beat until soft peaks form. When the sugar syrup is ready, slowly stream it into the egg whites (avoid hitting the beaters) while continuing to beat on medium speed. Then increase the speed to medium-high and beat until stiff peaks form. Spoon the meringue into a pastry bag fitted with a plain tip.

TO FINISH

Pipe puffs of the meringue onto the top of each yuzu. Lightly brown the meringue with a kitchen torch. Garnish with the gold leaf.

my first **EGG** was given to me AT A GAS STATION on the edge of **ANTWERP,** as a piece of **CONTRABAND**

Roger van Damme

Het Gebaar

Het Gebaar is closed during the evening hours yet has a Michelin star, which says a lot about just how good chef Roger van Damme is. In his extraordinary restaurant, the pastry chef serves a hearty lunch (think of fried veal and cannelloni filled with candied calf cheeks), but he owes his fame to desserts. Just like British chef Heston Blumenthal of The Fat Duck, Van Damme deconstructs classics such as *dame blanche* and gives his own twist with flavors like tonka bean, lemongrass, vanilla, and salt. His designs pay tribute to artists such as Roger Raveel, but also to Lego pieces as seen at the Brussels Atomium. "I really like forming little balls, quenelles, and small droplets."

Van Damme stresses the importance of aromas. "My father was a chef, and my grandfather was a baker. I remember smelling the first cookie coming out of the oven when I was young. That smell settled into my memory, leading me toward my first steps into the sweet culinary world. One of my children also has an amazing sense of smell; perhaps he will do something with it later on."

Roger finds his recipes all over the world. He recently returned from Bangkok and immediately began thinking about a new appetizer. In the future, he hopes to sell his wares under his own name to hotels and restaurants in the Thai capital. And if the venture succeeds, he'd also like to sell in Singapore and Hong Kong. "I can't sit still. When I'm not working, I ask myself, did I lose anything that day by doing nothing? But one has to rest the body; you have to be able to live. I'm afraid I live to work."

He learned to keep things as simple as possible from Gert Verhulst of Studio 100. "I also do a lot of programs for various television channels, such as njam! and 24Kitchen, so I have to keep it easy. I find it wonderful to share my knowledge with people, and if they use my ideas, I see it as a compliment."

According to Van Damme, a great dessert should be "creamy, yet crispy, and the main body should have the same melting point so that everything comes together in a taste explosion. The entire dessert must also have a nice balance to it."

Looking out at the adjacent herb garden in the heart of Antwerp, Van Damme (who grew up in Vlaanderen, Zeeland, but is a long-ago transplanted Dutchman in Belgium) remembers how he first learned about the Big Green Egg. "My first EGG was presented to me at a gas station, on the edge of Antwerp, as a piece of contraband. I met importer Wessel Buddingh at a world championship barbecue cook-off and we clicked."

You could call Roger van Damme an ambassador of the Big Green Egg. "I am always open to new things. If someone comes up with a revolutionary idea for a hand-towel drier, I will place an order. The same goes for the EGG. People don't associate pastry and desserts with a barbecue, but the EGG is a special oven that does amazing things. Even chocolate or cake works because you can control the temperature perfectly, and you can add wonderful aromas. A lightly smoked chocolate cake is sublime. Smoking things cold is amazing. First, bake the cake in a standard oven and then smoke it when it's cold—a perfect match!" Other examples include grilling sugar-laden fruits, which then caramelize. Pineapple, watermelon, and apples also lend themselves to grilling.

Tip: "Make sure your dish exudes love and share it with everyone. While you are cooking, your taste buds are warming up. Without smell and smoke, your dish will be literally tasteless."

www.hetgebaar.be

SERVES 4	COOKING TIME	GRILL TEMPERATURE	EQUIPMENT
	15 minutes	Set the EGG for direct cooking with	Cast Iron Grid
	(+ 20 minutes to infuse and 2 hours to	the Cast Iron Grid.	
	vacuum seal the fresh watermelon)	Preheat the EGG to 350°F (180°C).	

At Het Gebaar, this dessert includes an isomalt sugar ball filled with the raspberry *espuma*, as shown in the photograph. In this version, the *espuma* is released onto the surface of the gazpacho.

GRILLED WATERMELON with watermelon GAZPACHO

Ingredients

GRILLED WATERMELON
½ seedless watermelon

RASPBERRIES-ESPUMA
2 cups (500 g) raspberry purée
½ cup (125 ml) plus 6½ tablespoons (95 ml) water
½ cup (95 g) sugar
1 teaspoon unflavored gelatin

FRESH WATERMELON WITH
VACUUM-SEALED SUGAR WATER
2 cups (500 ml) water
⅔ cup (125 g) sugar
Juice of 1 lemon
4 lemongrass stalks
2 mint sprigs

GAZPACHO
1 cup (225 g) syrup
1½ cups (350 g) watermelon balls

Cherry tomatoes, for garnish
Pomelo flowers, for garnish

Preparation

GRILLED WATERMELON

Cut 2 or 3 thick slices of watermelon. Place the slices on the Cast Iron Grid, close the lid of the EGG, and cook on both sides to create grill marks and caramelize slightly. Remove the watermelon from the EGG, let cool, and cut into 1-inch (2.5-cm) cubes and into small rectangles. Set them aside. Using a melon baller, scoop balls from the remaining watermelon and reserve.

RASPBERRY ESPUMA

Combine the raspberry purée and the ½ cup (125 ml) water in a medium bowl. Combine the remaining 6½ tablespoons (95 ml) water and the sugar in a medium saucepan over high heat on the stove top and bring to a boil, stirring to dissolve the sugar. Remove from the heat, stir in the gelatin, and then add to the raspberry purée mixture, mixing well. Let cool completely. Pour the liquid into a siphon; charge the siphon with CO_2 cartridges and chill in the refrigerator for 30 minutes before dispensing.

FRESH WATERMELON WITH VACUUM-SEALED SUGAR WATER

Combine the water and sugar in a medium saucepan over high heat on the stove top and bring to a boil, stirring to dissolve the sugar. Remove from the heat and stir in the lemon juice, lemongrass, and mint sprigs. Cover with plastic wrap and let the mixture infuse for 20 minutes. Uncover, pour through a fine-mesh sieve into a medium bowl, and let cool. Place the watermelon balls and several tablespoons of the sugar syrup in a vacuum bag and seal. (Reserve the remaining sugar syrup for another use.) Let stand for at least 2 hours.

GAZPACHO

Empty the contents of the vacuum bag into a blender and process to a smooth purée.

TO FINISH

Place the serving dishes in the freezer for 30 minutes. Divide the gazpacho among the chilled serving dishes and add the watermelon balls. Garnish with cherry tomatoes and pomelo flowers. Shake the siphon vigorously, then release some of the espuma onto each serving.

a sunday in GIETHOORN a small boat, a tile to set the green egg on, and BOATING WE GO

Jonnie Boer
De Librije

In just over twenty years, Jonnie Boer and Thérèse Boer have reached culinary heights with their restaurant, De Librije. It continually ranks as one of the top one hundred restaurants in the world and for years has been awarded three Michelin stars. A second restaurant, Librije's Zusje, or Librije's Little Sister, received two stars in 2014. The couple's cooking "temples" have attracted guests from both home and abroad, and they can sleep off their gastronomical intoxication at the adjacent Librije's Hotel. Two restaurants, a hotel, a cooking studio, Food on Tour, and a shop make up the Boer empire. Mac van Dinther described Jonnie Boer's cooking style in the Dutch newspaper *Volkskrant* as "one with his environment, a down-home style not prone to pretense, yet seeing the need for finery."

The man who grew up in Giethoorn picks up fish from Urk, swears by the Dutch cheesemonger, obtains deer directly from the hunter, and picks his herbs from the ditch. In his book, *Puurst*, he added a thirty-five-page index of herbal plants and mushrooms. It is no wonder Boer found a "green" companion in horticulturist Eef Stel, who grows vegetables, herbs, and flowers exclusively for Boer in Dalfsen aan de Vecht. Boer says, "I believe in picking in the morning and serving it on your plate at night."

With his iPad in hand, he walks into De Librije early in the morning and is ready to talk about the barbecue phenomenon and the role the Big Green Egg plays. "We Dutch people don't have a barbecue tradition, although grilling is the epitome of slow cooking. Compare that to Australia! People here are more inclined to buy a cheap barbecue grill, throw on some starter, neatly line up charcoal, and cook their first pork chops. This method is guaranteed to give their food a petroleum taste—grilling can be done in a much better way. Give up on the idea of eating quickly. Dutch people want everything as fast as possible as far as cooking goes, which is too bad. They want to grill in a hurry. My father-in-law used to have a barbecue with an extension cord, so to get him to try the Big Green Egg was a real ordeal. I gave him one, and he never looked back. People need to take that first step, and then they will be richly rewarded.

"If Dutch people would realize what beautiful ingredients we have in our country, they would happily grill them on the Big Green Egg. Every night I have people eating at the chef's table. A culinary fanatic recently returned from Italy, where he had purchased porcini. He saw the Big Green Egg standing on the hearth at our restaurant, and he became very excited. I asked him, 'Do you know what we have here in the Netherlands? You don't have to go to Italy for porcini.' I went to the refrigerator and pulled out some porcini that I had purchased that morning. 'You know what,' I told him, 'let's skip the song and dance, and I'll make some porcini for you on the Big Green Egg.' He didn't understand what was going on. If he and his kids come here looking for porcini instead of going to Italy, in three hundred years, we'll have a new culinary tradition.

"I discovered the Big Green Egg about ten years ago. It was love at first sight, and I had to have one. I am a gadget man at heart, but the appliance has to serve a purpose. De Librije was one of the first restaurants in the Netherlands with an EGG. We have had dishes prepared with the Big Green Egg on the menu for over ten years.

"We started it up right away. Then we had breakfast next to an open-fire pit with burning birch wood chips filling the dome. When the wood chips were reduced to embers, we were ready to grill. At that time I was experimenting with wood chips and gale, a species of flowering plant that grows here in the region and is used in beer making. The taste is quite bitter, but the aroma is quite delicious. When you barbecue or grill with a mixture of wood chips and gale, you get a heavy cinnamon-like aroma. And if you barbecue sweetbreads, they will turn out delightful."

"A while back I had a boat in Giethoorn. On a Sunday, we would set the EGG on a stone tile and my wife, Thérèse, the kids, and I would go sailing while the Big Green Egg was cooking. We would fire it up in the morning, and four hours later we would be eating lobster or fish. When I am enjoying downtime with my family, I really go all out with the EGG."

Tip: "Don't stash it away in the closet, but experiment and use it as an oven. You can flavor vegetables, fruits, and even chocolate. You don't have to prepare each and every meal with the Big Green Egg. But you can add variety with different-flavored wood chips (see page 196). Sometimes it takes only a minute to get the flavor you want and other times it takes much longer. Throw on some sweet potatoes or eggplant and see what happens—brilliant! Or, put some celery root on the grid and grill until it is almost done. Let the EGG cool with the lid on and the temperature should stay at about 155°F (70°C). Press the juices from the not-quite-cooked celery root and pour the juice over some scallops."

www.librije.com

GRILL TEMPERATURE

Set the EGG for direct cooking without the grid. Preheat the EGG to 195°F (90°C).

EQUIPMENT

Handful of wood chips, soaked in water for at least 30 minutes
Small ovenproof saucepan
Half Moon Cast Iron Griddle (ridged side)

It was love at first sight for me and the Big Green Egg; I also had to have one on the hearth. De Librije was one of the first restaurants in the Netherlands with a Big Green Egg, and dishes cooked in the EGG have now been on the menu for more than ten years.

SCALLOPS WITH MARROW, smoked celery root bouillon AND MACADAMIA NUTS AND LAPSANG SOUCHONG

Ingredients

CELERY ROOT BOUILLON
2 celery roots
Salt
Pinch of xantana powder (binding agent; optional)

BLACK GARLIC PURÉE
2 to 3 tablespoons vegetable oil
15 cloves black garlic
1 clove garlic
1¼ cups (300 ml) chicken stock
1 tablespoon squid ink
Salt and cayenne pepper, for seasoning
2 teaspoons agar agar powder

CELERY ROOT PURÉE
½ celery root
3½ tablespoons heavy cream
1 tablespoon plus 2 teaspoons unsalted butter
Salt

MACADAMIA NUTS
3½ tablespoons celery root bouillon
½ cup (35 g) Lapsang souchong tea leaves
¾ cup (100 g) macadamia nuts
2 tablespoons unsalted butter

MARROW AND SCALLOPS
2 veal marrowbones
4 cups (960 ml) salted water (made with 3 tablespoons salt)
12 sea scallops
Coarse sea salt

Curry oil, for garnish
12 nasturtium leaves and / or flowers, for garnish

Preparation

CELERY ROOT BOUILLON

Peel the celery roots and pass them through a juice extractor. Transfer the juice to a small saucepan, place over high heat on the stove top, and boil until slightly thickened. Strain through a fine-mesh sieve lined with cheesecloth.

Season the bouillon with salt. Scatter the wood chips over the hot coals and place the cooking grid in the EGG. Pour half of the bouillon into the ovenproof saucepan and reserve the remaining bouillon for glazing the nuts later. Place the saucepan on the grid in the EGG, close the lid of the EGG, and smoke for 30 minutes. If the bouillon is very thin, use the xantana powder to thicken.

BLACK GARLIC PURÉE

Heat the oil in a medium frying pan over medium heat on the stove top. Add the black garlic and regular garlic and sauté for a few minutes, or until tender. Add the stock and cook for a few minutes until the liquid reduces and thickens. Remove from the heat, stir in the squid ink, and pour into a blender or small food processor. Process until a smooth purée forms. Season with salt and cayenne pepper. Transfer to a small saucepan, add the agar agar powder, and bring to a boil over high heat. Boil for 1 minute, then let cool completely. Set aside to cool, then pour into a squeeze bottle.

CELERY ROOT PURÉE

Peel the celery root and cut into chunks. Place in a steamer over simmering water and steam for about 20 minutes, or until tender. Let cool, then transfer to a blender, add the cream and butter, and process until a smooth purée forms. Season with the salt and pour the purée into a squeeze bottle for later use.

MACADAMIA NUTS

Bring the bouillon to a boil in a small saucepan over high heat on the stove top. Add the tea and remove from the heat. Let steep for about 10 minutes. Strain through a fine-mesh sieve into a clean small saucepan, add the nuts, and return to a boil. Add the butter and heat until the nuts are nicely glazed. Let the nuts cool for 35 to 45 minutes.

MARROW AND SCALLOPS

This step must be started a day in advance of serving. Immerse the marrowbones in the salted water in a covered container and refrigerate for 1 day. Drain the bones and then immerse them in a large bowl of lukewarm water (110° to 115°F/43°to 45°C) for about 5 minutes to soften the marrow slightly. Remove a bone from the water and, holding it over a plate, press against one end with your thumb to begin freeing the marrow. Continue with your thumb and then index finger until the marrow slides free. Repeat with the second bone. Using a

warm knife, slice the marrow into 12 tightly packed slices and then shape each slice into a round about the same diameter as a scallop.

Place the Half Moon Cast Iron Griddle, ridged side up, in the EGG, close the lid of the EGG, and preheat to 355° to 390°F (180° to 200°C). Place the scallops and marrow rounds on the hot Griddle,

close the lid of the EGG, and cook for 2 to 3 minutes on each side, until golden and lightly cooked. Remove the scallops and marrow from the EGG and sprinkle with coarse salt.

TO FINISH
Squeeze a round of celery root purée onto each plate. Place 3 slices of the marrow around the plate,

top each slice with a scallop, and dot the plate with droplets of the garlic purée. Ladle the smoked bouillon over the entire plate and add drops of curry oil. Garnish with the macadamia nuts (either on the side of the plate as a side garnish or under the leaves) and top with the nasturtium leaves and/or flowers.

EQUIPMENT

Handful of apple wood chips, soaked
in water for at least 30 minutes
convEGGtor
Baking dish
9-inch (23-cm) round cake pan

GRILL TEMPERATURE

Set the EGG for indirect cooking without the
convEGGtor.
Preheat the EGG to 250°F (120°C).

Using the Big Green Egg as an oven gives everything—
produce, fruit, chocolate—a unique flavor.

roasted
WHITE CHOCOLATE
with orange, dill,
AND PISTACHIO

Ingredients

WHITE CHOCOLATE CREAM

1 pound (450 g) white chocolate, chopped
3 lemongrass stalks
3 small gelatin sheets, 1 (0.25-ounce) envelope
granulated gelatin, or 1 tablespoon powdered gelatin
⅔ cup (150 ml) whole milk
1 cup (240 ml) heavy cream

PISTACHIO CAKE

⅔ cup (150 g) unsalted butter
⅔ cup (100 g) potato starch
⅔ cup (80 g) all-purpose flour
2½ cups (300 g) finely chopped pistachios
1¾ teaspoons salt
¾ teaspoon baking powder
⅔ cup (150 ml) pistachio oil
Grated zest and juice of 1 lemon
Grated zest and juice of 1 lime
3 eggs, lightly beaten
1 cup (200 g) sugar

LEMON BASE AND DILL-FLAVORED GELATIN

¾ cup (180 ml) fresh lemon juice
¾ cup (150 g) sugar
1⅔ cups (400 ml) water
Scant ½ cup (100 ml) apple cider
1½ tablespoons agar agar powder
½ teaspoon sodium citrate
Leaves from ½ bunch dill, finely chopped

ORANGE COMPOTE

4 oranges
1 tablespoon jelly sugar
Grated zest of ½ orange

Dill sprigs, for garnish

Preparation

WHITE CHOCOLATE CREAM

Scatter the wood chips over the hot coals, then place the convEGGtor, with legs facing up, in the EGG and top with the cooking grid. Place the white chocolate and lemongrass in the baking dish, place on the grid, and close the lid of the EGG. Caramelize the chocolate for 25 minutes. Set aside.

While the chocolate is caramelizing, soak the gelatin sheets in cold water for 5 to 10 minutes, until soft. (If using granulated or powdered gelatin, sprinkle it over a few tablespoons of cold water and let stand for 5 to 10 minutes, until dissolved.) Bring the milk to a boil in a small saucepan over high heat on the stove top and remove from the heat. Remove the gelatin sheets from the water, wringing out the excess water, and add to the hot milk. Stir until dissolved. (If using granulated sugar or powdered gelatin, add and stir to mix.)

Remove and discard the lemongrass from the caramelized chocolate, then stir the hot milk into the chocolate, mixing well. Pour through a sieve into a medium bowl. Let cool. Whisk the cream in a small bowl until it is the consistency of yogurt. Using a rubber spatula, fold the cream into the chocolate mixture. Cover and refrigerate to firm up.

PISTACHIO CAKE

Melt the butter in a small saucepan on the stove top over medium-low heat. When it starts to foam, stir it occasionally to prevent the milk solids from burning. Continue to heat until the butter has turned a pale nut brown and smells lightly nutty and toasty. Pour off the clear butter into a bowl, leaving the sediment behind, and let cool.

Increase the temperature of the EGG to 320°F (160°C). Butter the 9-inch (23-cm) round cake pan. In a bowl, stir together the potato starch, flour, pistachios, salt, and baking powder until thoroughly mixed. Add the browned butter, oil, and the lemon and lime zests and juices and mix well (this is the pistachio base). Measure 2⅓ cups (550 ml) of the pistachio base. Whisk together the eggs and sugar in a medium bowl until the sugar dissolves and the mixture lightens in color. Using a rubber spatula, fold the 2⅓ cups (550 ml) pistachio base into the egg mixture, mixing thoroughly. (You will end up with more pistachio base than you need for 1 cake, but you can save the base in the refrigerator for up to 2 days to make this dessert again.) Pour the mixture into the prepared pan. Place the pan on the cooking grid, close the lid of the EGG, and bake the cake for 20 to 25 minutes, until a skewer inserted into the center comes out clean. Let cool completely in the pan on a wire rack, then crumble the cake with your hands and set aside until ready to plate the dish.

LEMON BASE AND DILL-FLAVORED GELATIN

To make the lemon base, combine the lemon juice, sugar, and water in a medium saucepan, place over high heat on the stove top, and bring to a boil, stirring until the sugar dissolves. Remove from the heat. (You will end up with more lemon base than you need to make this

dessert, but you can save the base in the refrigerator for up to 2 days to make this dessert again.)

To make the dill gelatin, measure 1⅓ cups (315 ml) of the lemon base and place in a medium saucepan. Add the apple cider, agar agar powder, and sodium citrate, place the pan over high heat on the stove top, and bring to a boil. Boil for 1 minute, then pour into a shallow heatproof dish and set aside until cool and firmly set. Transfer the

gelatin to a blender and process until smooth. Add the dill and blend for a few more seconds. If the mixture is not completely smooth, run it through a sieve. Transfer to a squeeze bottle.

ORANGE COMPOTE
Peel the oranges and break into sections. Set aside half of the sections. Place the remaining sections in a medium saucepan, place over medium heat on the stove top, and bring to a boil. Boil for 1 minute, then

stir in the jelly sugar and boil for 1 minute longer. Remove the pan from the heat and add the reserved orange sections and the orange zest. Let cool.

TO FINISH
Spread the white chocolate cream on each serving plate. Sprinkle the cake crumbles in a line on the plate over the chocolate cream. Spoon the compote over the top and add dollops of the dill-flavored gelatin. Garnish with dill sprigs.

roasted white chocolate **BGE**

when you are GRILLING ON THE EGG good things are going TO HAPPEN

Martin Bosley

The Men in My Family Have Always Loved to Cook

When you are grilling on the Big GreenEgg . . . good things are going to be happening soon.

From the age of nine, Martin Bosley wanted to be a chef. "My parents dined out quite a bit," says Martin, "and my siblings and I often went along with them. On weekends, they hosted dinner parties that were largely influenced by their subscription to *Cordon Bleu* magazine. Each month when a new issue arrived, they would work their way through the magazine until they'd cooked every recipe. I soaked in all of this, and by the time I was a teenager, I could tell you the subtle differences between a profiterole and an éclair. Sunday afternoons, my father would lock himself in the kitchen and spend the day cooking . . . the men in my family have always loved to cook."

Martin has lived and worked most of his life in and around Wellington, New Zealand, a city he's passionate about for its proximity to the sea and to the rich vineyard and produce-growing regions of the country. He began his professional culinary career as an apprentice and went on to work in some of the most renowned restaurants and hotels in the country, landing his first head chef position at the age of twenty. In an amazingly short time, he established a reputation for innovation, gained a loyal following, and won the prestigious Best Restaurant in New Zealand award.

Living by the philosophy that we should eat what is in season, what is local, and what is fresh, Martin has garnered every major food award in New Zealand. Unequivocally committed to the region's culture, he is the cofounder of Wellington's iconic City Market, a weekly food and wine market showcasing culinary artisans and cuisines that reflect diverse tastes and stellar local produce.

Call it a barbie or a barbecue, the act of cooking outside is an essential slice of the New Zealand culture and a culinary experience that epitomizes the easy New Zealand lifestyle. "When you are grilling on the EGG with natural lump charcoal as the secret ingredient, you hear that lovely sizzling noise coming through. That tells me that the food and the EGG are talking to each other and that good things are going to be happening here soon."

www.martin-bosley.com

SERVES 4

COOKING TIME

1 hour

(+ 30 minutes to marinate)

GRILL TEMPERATURE

Set the EGG for direct cooking.

Preheat the EGG to 350°F (180°C).

EQUIPMENT

Dutch Oven or ovenproof saucepan

Instant-read thermometer

Yogurt, lemons, garlic, and rosemary are all the seasoning the lamb needs. You could easily replace the chops with leg of lamb, leg steaks, or cubed meat.

marinated LAMB CHOPS with red sauce

Ingredients

RED SAUCE

Olive oil, for cooking

2 cloves garlic, chopped

1 red chile, seeded and chopped finely

Leaves from 4 marjoram sprigs

1 (28-ounce/800-g) can whole tomatoes, drained and coarsely chopped

2 red bell peppers, seeded and finely chopped

Salt

Pinch of sweet paprika

LAMB

4 thick lamb chops

Olive oil, for rubbing

Salt and freshly ground black pepper

4 cloves garlic, chopped

4 rosemary sprigs

Juice of 1 lemon

Pita bread, for serving

Preparation

RED SAUCE

Lightly coat the bottom of the Dutch Oven or saucepan with oil and add the garlic. Place on the cooking grid, close the lid of the EGG, and cook for a few minutes, or until the garlic begins to color. Add the chile, marjoram, and tomatoes to the Dutch Oven, close the lid of the EGG, and cook for about 30 minutes, or until reduced and thickened. Add the bell peppers, close the lid of the EGG, and cook for 10 minutes longer, or until the bell peppers are tender. Remove the sauce from the EGG, season with salt and paprika, and let cool.

LAMB

Rub the lamb chops with a little oil, season with salt and pepper, and coat with the garlic. Place the chops in a shallow dish. Bruise the rosemary with the back of a kitchen knife and toss gently through the chops. Squeeze the lemon juice over the top, cover, and refrigerate for 30 minutes. Meanwhile, increase the temperature of the EGG to 425°F (220°C).

Place the lamb chops on the cooking grid, close the lid of the EGG, and cook for 6 to 8 minutes, until browned. Turn the chops over, close the lid again, and cook for a few minutes longer, until the chops are good and crusty on the outside and a soft pink on the inside, or the instant-read thermometer inserted into a chop away from bone registers 145°F (63°C) for medium-rare. Set the lamb aside to rest for a few minutes before serving.

TO FINISH

Serve the lamb with the red sauce and pita bread.

EGG
MODELS

MINI

A Mini EGG is perfect as a companion to other EGGs in an outdoor kitchen and as a portable solution for picnics and tailgating when you want to take The Ultimate Cooking Experience with you!

MINIMAX™

Designed with the height of a Mini yet all the volume capabilities of a Small ... the MiniMax EGG comes complete with its own Carrier and will delight you with oversized results in a small package!

SMALL

The Small EGG is an easy fit for patios and balconies and can be used along with a larger EGG to allow the preparation of several courses at once.

MEDIUM

Happiness in a more compact package—the Medium EGG is perfectly sized for smaller families and couples.

LARGE

The Large EGG is the most popular size and a favorite to handle the cooking needs of most families and gatherings of friends.

XLARGE

An XLarge EGG accommodates cookouts with all your friends and family—and you can efficiently prepare several meals over the coals at once.

XXLARGE

The unrivaled XXLarge EGG can easily handle your family reunion or cookouts with large groups—and is large enough to satisfy restaurant and catering needs.

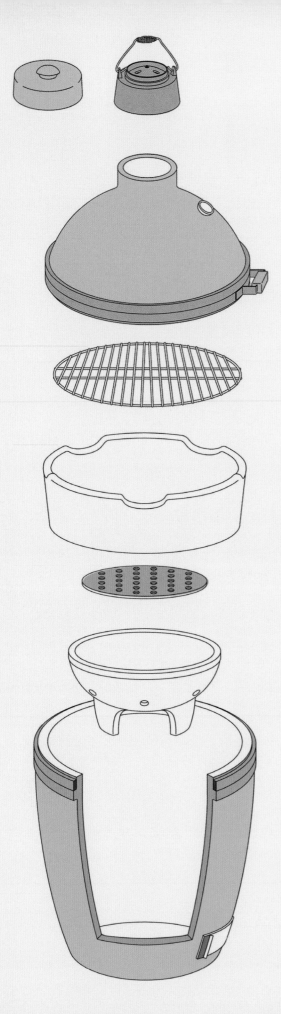

EGG BASICS

COMPONENTS OF THE EGG

An adjustable, patented stainless steel Draft Door, or air vent, is located near the base of the EGG. The Dual-Function Metal Top, a daisy-wheel-type air vent, sits on the chimney on the domed lid. This second vent can be fully closed with the Ceramic Damper Lid.

On all models except the Mini, the lid is connected to the base with rear-mounted heavy-duty, spring-loaded hinges that prevent the lid from closing too hard.

A temperature gauge on the domed lid provides an accurate reading of the temperature inside the EGG to 750°F (400°C).

The rim of both the base and the lid is lined with a heavy-duty gasket that seals heat inside the cooking chamber.

A Ceramic Fire Box and Fire Ring support the Fire Grate and the cooking grid. A heavy-duty stainless steel cooking grid is standard equipment; a cast iron cooking grid is available as an option.

BASIC NECESSITIES

BIG GREEN EGG ORGANIC CHARCOAL

The use of all-natural lump hardwood charcoal is essential to preparing foods with great flavor and to reaching and maintaining an optimum cooking temperature. Big Green Egg organic lump charcoal is made up of a perfect blend of two organic woods, oak and hickory. These select pieces burn hotter, cleaner, longer, and with less ash than standard charcoal briquettes, which contain chemicals, create hard-to-control fires, and can clog air vents.

BIG GREEN EGG CHARCOAL STARTERS

Big Green Egg Natural Charcoal Starters are small compressed sawdust and parafin blocks that contain no chemicals and emit no unpleasant odor or taste. Never use newspapers, chemical fire starters, or lighter fluid to start the EGG. They will create smoke, an unpleasant odor, and chemical residue. If your Big Green Egg is near an electrical outlet, you can use the Electric Charcoal Starter to get your fire going without even striking a match.

USING THE EGG

LIGHTING THE FIRE

Remove the Ceramic Damper Top from the EGG and replace it with the Dual-Function Metal Top, then fully open the Draft Door. Next, open the lid and remove the stainless steel cooking grid. Fill the Fire Box with natural lump charcoal almost to its rim. When cooking at an average temperature, you can expect a fully loaded Fire Box to burn for several hours. For longer cooking times, you can add more coals beneath the cooking grid, slipping them in alongside the hot coals, which will ignite them. When cooking at lower temperatures, a fully loaded Fire Box will sometimes burn for eighteen hours without having to add more charcoal.

Slip a charcoal starter block into the center of the charcoal and light it with a long match or a long-handled grill lighter, then replace the cooking grid. When several coals are burning, usually after about 10 minutes, close the dome and fully open the Dual-Function Metal Top until the desired temperature is reached.

If using the Electrical Charcoal Starter, plug in the starter and then bury its coil in the charcoal. As the coil becomes hot, it ignites the surrounding charcoal within about 7 minutes. Once the coals are burning, unplug the starter and carefully set it on its positioning bracket to cool, then close the dome and, as with the Natural Charcoal Starter, fully open the Dual-Function Metal Top until the desired temperature is reached.

REGULATING THE TEMPERATURE

To maintain the desired temperature, adjust the Dual-Function Metal Top and the Draft Door to reduce airflow, using the vent on the dome to fine-tune the temperature. Once the temperature is steady, you can start cooking.

Temperature regulation takes some practice. Is the temperature too low? If so, increase the air circulation by opening the air vents a little more. Once the EGG is going, keep the lid closed as much as possible. The heat will be more uniform, less fuel will be used, and foods will retain more moisture and thus flavor. Also, with the lid closed, it is easier to regulate the temperature with the top and base vents (the more air, the higher the temperature).

"BURPING" THE EGG

Always use caution when opening the EGG if cooking at temperatures above 300°F (150°C). Lift the lid no more than 2 inches (5 cm) and then stop for a few seconds to "burp" it before continuing to open the lid fully. This two-step process allows the rush of oxygen to burn safely inside the chamber, eliminating the possibility of a backdraft or flare-up that can cause injury.

TO EXTINGUISH

When you have finished cooking, it is easy to extinguish the fire in the Big Green Egg. Simply close the air vent in the base and the vent in the lid (or top the lid with the Ceramic Damper Cap). This will put out the fire relatively quickly and preserve any unburned charcoal for another time. (Be sure to rake these old coals across the Fire Grate to release any ash into the bottom of the EGG before adding more charcoal and lighting a new fire.) In the first 5 minutes after closing the vents, do not open the lid too quickly, as the resulting oxygen intake can cause flare-ups. Let the EGG sit for a full day before removing the ash, to make sure it is completely cooled.

COOKING TECHNIQUES

More than just a grill, the Big Green Egg offers cooking flexibility, flavor, and juiciness second to none. Here is a sampling of what you can accomplish in the EGG.

DIRECT GRILLING

For direct grilling, food is placed over the fire and cooked by direct exposure to the flame and heat. Direct grilling with the Big Green Egg creates a delicious crusty exterior and a surprisingly soft, tender interior with the juices locked inside. Because of the ingenious design of the EGG and the fact that grilling is always done with the lid closed, flare-ups and hot spots are virtually eliminated. Generally, foods that are tender, less than two inches thick, and boneless are good candidates for direct grilling. It is ideal for chops, steaks, burgers, boneless chicken breasts, kabobs, fish fillets, certain vegetables, and other quick-cooking foods. And with a Stir-Fry and Paella Grill Pan in place directly over the hot fire, you can even make a tasty stir-fry.

Some foods call for starting over a very high temperature to achieve a well-seared exterior and then lowering the temperature to finish cooking. The standard stainless steel cooking grid is good for grilling fish, some meats, and other foods. The Cast Iron Grid (see page 197) is recommended for red meats and poultry, as it leaves the characteristic grill marks. The Half Moon Cast Iron Griddle (see page 198) is ideal for smaller foods that may be lost through the slats of a grid.

INDIRECT GRILLING AND ROASTING

In indirect grilling and roasting, the food is not directly exposed to the flames and heat of the fire. Rather, a shield such as a Roasting & Drip Pan or convEGGtor is placed beneath the food to deflect the heat. Food is cooked by convection heat—actually the heated air and radiant heat, which reflects off the coals, side walls, and lid of the EGG. In addition, once the dampers are adjusted to the desired temperature, the charcoal fire will burn steadily for hours without requiring frequent tending or replenishing.

Indirect grilling or roasting is best for larger cuts of meat such as turkeys, chickens, roasts, and hams, which take longer to cook. In general, use this method to cook anything thicker than two inches or with a bone, such as chicken pieces; otherwise the exterior will be charred before the interior is cooked through. One exception to this would be bone-in steaks, such as T-bone or porterhouse, which are best grilled directly over the fire.

SMOKING

Cooking slowly over low heat infused with wood smoke is what smoking—and what some call "real barbecue"—is all about. Cooking "low and slow" is the only way to break down connective tissue and tenderize tough (and typically less expensive) cuts of meat like beef brisket, pork shoulder, pork butts, and spare ribs. For smoking these kinds of foods, cooking times are measured in hours rather than minutes. But boy, is it worth it! The result is succulent, fall-off-the-bone tenderness with the tangy, complex combination of spices, smoke, and natural meat flavors. Of course, you can also smoke other types of foods that do not fit the standard profile. Fish, turkey, nuts, vegetables, and even cheeses do not need to be tenderized with slow cooking, but they taste even better when kissed with the essence of wood smoke.

The Big Green Egg is ideal for smoking both individual foods and complete dishes because the EGG makes temperature control easy. True smoking temperatures generally range from 225° to 275°F (107° to 135°C). Once you get the hang of it, it's a piece of cake to adjust the draft openings to set the proper temperature. But unlike a true pitmaster, who must work hard to maintain those low temperatures steadily throughout the extended smoking period, an EGG can retain heat at precise temperatures for many hours of cooking with little attention required.

The convEGGtor (see page 194) also makes smoking in the EGG efficient and easy, because it acts as a shield between the food and the direct heat of the fire, but allows the smoke and hot air to circulate freely around the food. In addition, it eliminates the need to turn food during the smoking process.

For the best results, use only wood chips or chunks for smoking, avoiding sawdust or other wood products. The Big Green Egg has its own line of aromatic wood chips and chunks, including apple, pecan, cherry, hickory, and mesquite, which can be used as is for a milder flavor or soaked in water for at least thirty minutes before use for a more intense smoke.

To use the chips or chunks, once the EGG has reached the desired cooking temperature, remove the cooking grid from the EGG, sprinkle the chips directly on the glowing embers, and then, if using the convEGGtor, set it, with the legs facing up, in the EGG. If a Roasting & Drip Pan is called for in the recipe, place it on the convEGGtor. Replace the cooking grid, put the food to be smoked on the grid, close the lid, and start smoking. The size and type of food and personal taste will determine smoking times and core temperatures. Most foods are smoked at temperatures ranging from 225° to 275°F (110° to 135°C).

If you have something on your menu that calls for a long, slow smoke, you can alternate layers of lump charcoal and wood chips in the Fire Box to guarantee plenty of smoke flavor throughout the process. Start with a layer of charcoal and scatter a small handful of wood chips over the top. Repeat the layers until you reach the rim of the Fire Box.

Here are a handful of tips on pairing different types of wood chips with specific foods.

- Apple: pork, chicken, turkey, sausage, ham
- Cherry: lamb, duck, game birds, game such as venison
- Mesquite: beef, lamb, pork, game
- Oak: fish, ham, pork sausages
- Pecan and hickory: smoky, spicy dishes, especially classic American barbecue recipes

BAKING

The EGG, with its unique ceramic construction, superior heat retention, and precision temperature control, is also the perfect "oven" for baking. With the addition of a convEGGtor and a Pizza & Baking Stone, your ceramic cooker becomes a classic brick oven that bakes beautifully browned loaves of breads, biscuits, pies, pizzas, cobblers, cookies, and cakes. As pizza cooks, moisture is drawn to the Stone for an authentic, crispy, brick-oven-style crust that is impossible to re-create in an indoor oven or on an ordinary barbecue grill. As with the surfaces used in direct grilling, always preheat the Pizza & Baking Stone in the EGG before sliding a pizza or bread onto it.

COOKING WITH WOOD PLANKS

Cooking on wood planks, a technique borrowed from Native Americans, infuses fish and meats with a subtle smokiness and wood-scented flavor. The plank must be submerged in water for at least 1 hour before use. Then, when ready to cook, place the plank on the cooking grid of the preheated EGG, close the lid, leave for a few minutes to heat, and then flip the plank, place the food to be cooked on the now-heated side, and close the lid. The food can then be cooked without flipping it again. Cedar and red oak are two popular woods used for planks.

EGGCESSORIES

convEGGtor

The three-legged ceramic convEGGtor is used for indirect cooking on the Big Green Egg, providing a barrier between the food and direct heat, turning your EGG into a convection oven. Paired with the Pizza & Baking Stone, and positioned with the legs facing up or down, it is ideal for baking pizzas, calzone, tarts, and breads. With only the grid or with the grid and a V-Rack or Roasting & Drip Pan, it is used for roasting meats and poultry. It is also ideal for baked dishes, cooked in a Dutch Oven or baking dish.

CAST IRON GRID

For perfect sear marks on your food, utilize the superior heat conductivity of the Cast Iron Grid as an alternative to the primary Stainless Cooking Grid. The cast iron gets very hot and retains the heat, turning it into a perfect searing surface. Flip the grid over for a flat searing surface for fish or seafood.

PERFORATED COOKING GRID

Available in round and half moon shapes, the Perforated Cooking Grids are ideal for direct cooking of small foods, such as mushrooms, shrimp, or any food that may slip between the bars of a standard cooking grid.

PERFORATED GRILL WOK

Like the Perforated Cooking Grids, the Perforated Grill Wok eliminates the possibility of losing small foods through the slats of a cooking grid. The Grill Wok allows the heat and smoke to circulate around food for even cooking and flavor absorbtion.

STIR-FRY AND PAELLA GRILL PAN

This large (4-quart/3.8-L) stainless steel pan is perfect for whipping up stir-frys and paella and also for simmering big sauces.

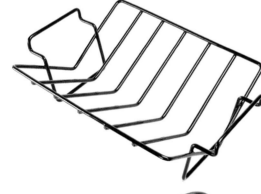

DUTCH OVEN

This 5-quart (4.7-L) cast iron pot with lid is highly versatile, ideal for cooking everything from vegetables to meats to a loaf of bread or a fruit cobbler.

VERTICAL ROASTERS

Available in three styles (metal frame, ceramic, and folding), the Vertical Roaster guarantees a perfectly roasted chicken or turkey every time. The bird sits upright on the Roaster, which fits snugly inside the cavity, ensuring even browning and crisp skin. A Roasting & Drip Pan can be used with the Roaster to catch drippings that can be used to baste the bird or to hold beer, juice, or other liquid that will infuse the bird as it cooks.

V-RACKS

These porcelain-coated racks, which come in two sizes, large and small, are dual purpose. Positioned right side up, they will hold a large roast or a couple of chickens, and they can be matched with a Roasting & Drip Pan to capture any drippings. When turned over, the V-Rack is perfect for holding racks of ribs vertically between the bars for slow roasting.

ROASTING & DRIP PANS

Available in two shapes, round and rectangular, these nonstick pans are used both under the grid to catch drippings and on the grid in combination with Vertical Roasters and V-Racks.

HALF MOON CAST IRON GRIDDLE

This versatile tool is outfitted with a smooth side and a ridged side. The smooth side is perfect for cooking pancakes, crepes, or eggs, and the ridged side is ideal for grilled sandwiches or delicate fish fillets. It goes directly atop the cooking grid, leaving half of the grid free for direct cooking. Or, you can pair two Griddles in the EGG or one Griddle and a Half Moon Cast Iron Grid.

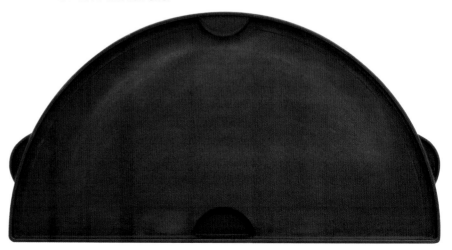

PIZZA & BAKING STONES

These heavy, thick ceramic stones, which sit atop the cooking grid, come in various forms. Pizza & Baking Stones, ideal for baking pizzas, calzone, breads, and other baked goods, come in two shapes, round (in three sizes) and half moon (in two sizes). The latter allows you to bake bread while roasting meat or other food on the grid. The 14-inch (35-cm) Deep Dish Pizza/Baking Stone is good for baking pies, tarts, deep-dish pizzas, and other dishes.

PIZZA ACCESSORIES

The silicone Dough Rolling Mat makes rolling out pizza and calzone dough fast and easy.

Two Pizza Peels are available, wood and aluminum. Both simplify lifting a pizza or calzone (or a loaf of bread) into and out of the EGG.

The calzone, a popular folded pizza, is effortlessly made with the Italian Calzone Press. You just place the rolled out dough on the Press, add the filling, and close the Press, sealing the edges of the calzone.

Ready to serve your pizza? First, slide it onto a cutting board, then use the Rolling Pizza Cutter, which slices cleanly through even thicker crusts without disturbing the toppings. Or, use the Rockin' Pizza Cutter, a slightly curved blade designed to cut through crispy or thick dough in one simple motion. Now, use the Pizza Slice Server to move the wedges easily onto plates or napkins.

GRID LIFTERS AND GRILL MITTS

The Big Green Egg has two specially designed lifters, the Grill Gripper and the Grid Lifter, that make removing hot cooking grids safe and simple. The Grilling Mitt and the Pit Mitt® BBQ Glove are indispensable for protecting hands when moving hot pans, stones, and other hot items in and out of the EGG.

THERMOMETERS

A variety of Big Green Egg thermometers, including a "Quick Read" Pocket Thermometer and an Instant Read Digital Thermometer, come in handy when cooking meat or poultry to safely monitor the internal temperature.

The Dual Probe Remote Wireless Thermometer monitors food temperatures from a distance of up to 300 feet (91m), and includes preset temperatures for beef, veal, lamb, pork and poultry ... and nine popular game meats.

The BBQ Guru, an automatic temperature control device, is equipped with microprocessor technology that enables chefs to automatically control the internal temperature of the EGG while monitoring the temperature of the meat being cooked. Set the temperature and forget it; you can relax by the pool or sleep soundly during a sixteen-hour low and slow cook.

OTHER TOOLS

The Chef's Flavor Injector is used to inject marinades, basting mixtures, and other liquids into meats and poultry to add flavor and moisture. Flexible Skewers are handy for direct cooking of meats, vegetables, and seafood, and Meat Claws make quick work of shredding pork, poultry, or other meats for sandwiches or other uses.

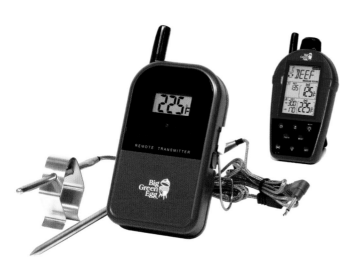

Metric Conversions and Equivalents

METRIC CONVERSION FORMULAS

TO CONVERT	MULTIPLY
Ounces to grams	Ounces by 28.35
Pounds to kilograms	Pounds by .454
Teaspoons to milliliters	Teaspoons by 4.93
Tablespoons to milliliters	Tablespoons by 14.79
Fluid ounces to milliliters	Fluid ounces by 29.57
Cups to milliliters	Cups by 236.59
Cups to liters	Cups by .236
Pints to liters	Pints by .473
Quarts to liters	Quarts by .946
Gallons to liters	Gallons by 3.785
Inches to centimeters	Inches by 2.54

COMMON INGREDIENTS AND THEIR APPROXIMATE EQUIVALENTS

1 cup all-purpose flour = 140 grams

1 stick butter (4 ounces • ½ cup • 8 tablespoons) = 110 grams

1 cup butter (8 ounces • 2 sticks • 16 tablespoons) = 220 grams

1 cup brown sugar, firmly packed = 225 grams

1 cup granulated sugar = 200 grams

APPROXIMATE METRIC EQUIVALENTS

VOLUME

¼ teaspoon	1 milliliter
½ teaspoon	2.5 milliliters
¾ teaspoon	4 milliliters
1 teaspoon	5 milliliters
1¼ teaspoons	6 milliliters
1½ teaspoons	7.5 milliliters
1¾ teaspoons	8.5 milliliters
2 teaspoons	10 milliliters
1 tablespoon (½ fluid ounce)	15 milliliters
2 tablespoons (1 fluid ounce)	30 milliliters
¼ cup	60 milliliters
⅓ cup	80 milliliters
½ cup (4 fluid ounces)	120 milliliters
⅔ cup	160 milliliters
¾ cup	180 milliliters
1 cup (8 fluid ounces)	240 milliliters
1¼ cups	300 milliliters
1½ cups (12 fluid ounces)	360 milliliters
1⅔ cups	400 milliliters
2 cups (1 pint)	460 milliliters
3 cups	700 milliliters
4 cups (1 quart)	0.95 liter
1 quart plus ¼ cup	1 liter
4 quarts (1 gallon)	3.8 liters

LENGTH

⅛ inch	3 millimeters
¼ inch	6 millimeters
½ inch	1¼ centimeters
1 inch	2½ centimeters
2 inches	5 centimeters
2½ inches	6 centimeters
4 inches	10 centimeters
5 inches	13 centimeters
6 inches	15¼ centimeters
12 inches (1 foot)	30 centimeters

WEIGHT

¼ ounce	7 grams
½ ounce	14 grams
¾ ounce	21 grams
1 ounce	28 grams
1¼ ounces	35 grams
1½ ounces	42.5 grams
1⅔ ounces	45 grams
2 ounces	57 grams
3 ounces	85 grams
4 ounces (¼ pound)	113 grams
5 ounces	142 grams
6 ounces	170 grams
7 ounces	198 grams
8 ounces (½ pound)	227 grams
16 ounces (1 pound)	454 grams
35.25 ounces (2.2 pounds)	1 kilogram

OVEN TEMPERATURES

To convert Fahrenheit to Celsius, subtract 32 from Fahrenheit, multiply the result by 5, then divide by 9.

DESCRIPTION	FAHRENHEIT	CELSIUS	BRITISH GAS MARK
Very cool	200°	95°	0
Very cool	225°	110°	¼
Very cool	250°	120°	½
Cool	275°	135°	1
Cool	300°	150°	2
Warm	325°	165°	3
Moderate	350°	175°	4
Moderately hot	375°	190°	5
Fairly hot	400°	200°	6
Hot	425°	220°	7
Very hot	450°	230°	8
Very hot	475°	245°	9

Information compiled from a variety of sources, including *Recipes into Type* by Joan Whitman and Dolores Simon (Newton, MA: Biscuit Books, 1993); *The New Food Lover's Companion* by Sharon Tyler Herbst (Hauppauge, NY: Barron's, 2013); and *Rosemary Brown's Big Kitchen Instruction Book* (Kansas City, MO: Andrews McMeel, 1998).

LISTING OF RECIPES AND CHEFS

INDEX

Andrews McMeel Publishing, LLC
1130 Walnut Street, Kansas City, Missouri 64106
www.andrewsmcmeel.com

BIG GREEN EGG, EGG, The Ultimate Cooking Experience, Prepare to Get Hungry, EGGhead, EGGfest, EGGcessories, EGGtoberfest, convEGGtor and EGG Mates are registered trademarks of The Big Green Egg, Inc.

Nest and MiniMax EGG are trademarks of The Big Green Egg, Inc. The particular green color and overall configuration of the cooker in this color are also trademarks of The Big Green Egg, Inc.

First published in 2013 by KOMMA/d'jonge Hond

© 2013, 2015 Big Green Egg

15 16 17 18 19 SDB 10 9 8 7 6 5 4 3 2 1

ISBN: 978-1-4494-7115-6

Library of Congress Control Number: 2015941166

Photography: **Remko Kraaijeveld**
Art direction, design: **Ronald Timmermans**
Recipes and food styling: **Vanja van der Leeden**
Chief recipe editor: **Vanja van der Leeden**
Recipe editor: **Rob van Riet**
Editors: **Dirk Koppes and Vanja van der Leeden**
Production supervisors: **Steven Hond, Ronald Timmermans**
Lithography and software: **Jan van der Meijde, Henk Tijbosch, Jan Hoogendijk RGM**
Biographies: **Dirk Koppes**
Biography editor: **Caroline Griep**

ANDREWS MCMEEL PUBLISHING, LLC
Editor: **Jean Z. Lucas**
Art director: **Diane Marsh**
Copy chief: **Maureen Sullivan**
Production manager: **Cliff Koehler**
Demand planner: **Sue Eikos**

Pages 146–47 reprinted with permission from *Big Green Egg Life Style* magazine, "Destination: South Africa," Reuben Riffel, v. 5 2015, 22–23.

Pages 168–71 reprinted with permission from *Big Green Egg Life Style* magazine, "Raghavan Iyer: A Cuisine of Spices," Raghavan Iyer, v. 4 2014, 16–17. Recipe p. 171 reprinted with permission of the author from Indian Cooking Unfolded (2013), by Raghavan Iyer. Published by Workman Publishing Co., Inc.

Pages 188–90 reprinted with permission from *Big Green Egg Life Style* magazine, "Destination: New Zealand," Martin Bosley, v. 5 2015, 30–31.

Attention: Schools and Businesses

Andrews McMeel books are available at quantity discounts with bulk purchase for educational, business, or sales promotional use. For information, please e-mail the Andrews McMeel Publishing Special Sales Department: specialsales@amuniversal.com